Christian Meditation
and Inner Healing

*For my parents,
Marvin and Murlene Judy.*

*They dared to pray
in an age of disbelief.*

Christian Meditation and Inner Healing

Dwight H. Judy

OSL Publications
Akron Ohio

Christian Meditation and Inner Healing

ISBN 1-878009-38-9

This book is printed on acid-free paper that meets the
American National Standards Institute Z39.48 Standard

Produced and manufactured in the United States of America by
OSL Publications
P. O. Box 22279
Akron, Ohio 44302-0079

Cover photography by Barbara Teague

Biblical quotations, unless otherwise noted, are from the New Revised Standard Version of the Bible, © 1989 Division of Christian Education of the National Council of the Churches of Christ in the United States of America.

Scripture quotations noted RSV are from the Revised Standard Version of the Bible, copyright 1946, 1952, © 1971, 1973 by the Division of Christian Education of the National Council fo the Churches of Christ in the U.S.A. and are used by permission.

Scripture quotations noted NEB are from The New English Bible © the Delegates of the Oxford University Press and the Syndics of the Cambridge University Press 1961, 1970. Reprinted by permission.

The Order of Saint Luke is a religious order dedicated to sacramental and liturgical scholarship, education and practice. The purpose of the publishing ministry is to put into the hands of students and practitioners resources which have theological, historical, ecumenical and practical integrity.

Contents

Foreword

A restless and pervasive hunger for a living spirituality has led many contemporary seekers to explore new religious movements, Eastern traditions, and psychotherapeutic techniques. Among those who have traveled these paths, some have found a way to integrate their expanded awareness of spiritual realities with their traditional spiritual roots. Dwight Judy's writing of *Christian Meditation and Inner Healing* is the fruit of a long and arduous personal journey in which his unswerving commitment to truth and the pursuit of wholeness led him to gather wisdom from many sources.

In a time when our culture is plagued by alienation, fear, and despair in the face of overwhelming global problems of catastrophic proportions, the need for spiritual nourishment and renewal is enormous. Without inner healing of the psyche, the world cannot hope for external healing. As we develop greater awareness of the role of human behavior in creating problems of pollution, overpopulation, depletion of resources, war, and social injustice, we recognize that inner work and social action are but two sides of one coin. Healing the earth depends on healing ourselves, and vice versa. This book offers us a way to begin.

Christians of all denominations will find that these guided meditations can enrich their spiritual life and assist them on the path of self-discovery. Many of the themes will be familiar, others new and challenging. By learning to understand the language of dreams and imagery in the process of recovering the soul, we are led through a maze of pathways in the imaginal realms to those images that can be most helpful for healing and wholeness. Mental health professionals who recognize the necessity of integrating spiritual issues with clinical practice will find this a valuable resource for working within a Christian framework and revitalizing a healthy spiritual orientation. Practical methods for integrating basic principles of transpersonal psychology with contemplative practice bring fresh inspiration to anyone seeking to deepen the spiritual life within the Christian tradition.

This book is easily comprehensible to any sincere seeker. By developing awareness of inner resources and divine guidance, one learns to cultivate a personal relationship to the inner teachers that facilitate access to wisdom. Those who are familiar with the presence of the Holy Spirit or the inner Christ may find many of these exercises helpful in deepening their contemplative practice. Those who have left institutional Christian religion in search of different approaches to the inner life may discover a way of reconnecting to their roots in a meaningful way.

This is a book to be experienced and savored, not just read. A casual reading is informative, but an immersion in the suggested meditations can be transformative. Many of the prayers and processes point to ways of healing the wounded psyche by illuminating the spiritual depths of our being. We are not asked to believe, but to experience, in a profound and significant way, the fruit of ancient teachings in a context that makes them relevant to contemporary life.

Drawing on both Eastern and Western sources of wisdom, and integrating personal work with a better understanding of the relationship between prayer and meditation, Dwight Judy dispels the illusion that psychological and spiritual work are unconnected. The unique combination of transpersonal psychological theory with Christian theology and mysticism gives us a better understanding of the relationship of psychological health to spiritual awakening and points the way to personal integration and wholeness. Both Christians and non-Christians will find this book illuminating. May it be read by many, for the benefit of all.

Frances Vaughan

Preface to OSL Edition

In February of 1979, the "silence of God" descended upon me. It was a time of great inner distress, a time when professional and personal values came into question. It was the beginning of my discovery that contemplative silence does not necessarily mean that we hear nothing, but rather, that in silence we may begin to hear everything.

From 1971 to 1979, I served as pastor of St. Stephen United Methodist Church in Mesquite, Texas, a suburb of Dallas. During my last year there, a change was awakening in me, a desire for listening more deeply to inward awarenesses. My need to heal my own psychological, spiritual, and physical distresses began to emerge. The congregation was generous with me as I struggled to discern my next step. An odyssey began. I was blessed by family and friends, and especially by the companionship of my wife, Ruth. She, too, was feeling the need for new exploration and deepening inner awareness. We found our way into the doctoral program of the Institute of Transpersonal Psychology, now located in Palo Alto, California, as a means of learning the tools of inner awareness emerging from psychology, body-mind relationships, and spiritual traditions. Together, Ruth and I made a profound inner pilgrimage, each learning to listen to the depths of the psyche and spirit more clearly, and each seeking to discern our own spiritual tasks.

I was especially privileged to "take home" much of my own learning as I directed a program in spiritual formation for Perkins School of Theology Continuing Education at Southern Methodist University in Dallas from 1984 to 1987. In those early years of my teaching, I was also privileged to begin teaching occasionally with Garrett-Evangelical Theological Seminary in Evanston, IL, a relationship that has continued to the present. Over the last twenty years, I have also been able to share the life of inner development and methods of meditative prayer practice with many clergy and lay people in numerous retreat settings throughout the country.

In ways that I could not understand at the time, I have held one foot in the world of transpersonal psychology over the years, and the other in the life of the church. I had some affiliation with the Institute of Transpersonal Psychology, first a doctoral student, then as Associate Professor and Chair of the External Division, from 1980 until 1994. Many of the ideas and methods of this book were tested within that learning community for several years in classes I taught on Christian mysticism and on psychology of meditation. Since 1980, I have also shared these methods in church-related retreat settings.

I have spent the last twenty years studying and teaching the ways of silence as a teacher, retreat guide, and spiritual director. This book is a collection of thoughts and methods that I have discovered from Christian tradition, woven together with images of the human psyche from the field of transpersonal psychology. In an era when many people are searching for more authentic lives rooted in a contemplative understanding of themselves, I hope that this book will provide some guidance. We are at a very exciting juncture in which the ancient practices of contemplative Christianity have been recovered and can now dialogue with such practices from other religious traditions and with a culture more attuned to the transpersonal domain of the psyche.

As I began this process of inner growth for myself, I was captivated by one particular image from Jesus' teaching: the image of "living water." I likened my first education in college and seminary as filling my cup to the brim. During that first decade of ministry, I felt that I had poured out and emptied my cup. From that place of profound emptiness, I sought to discover a different way of learning and being and listening for divine direction. I sought the source of "living water." I sought to cleanse my own perception of reality so that there might awaken a constant awareness of God. What I could not have predicted is that in following the inner leadership to be still, I would discover a life work - the sharing of contemplative Christianity. In 1993, I had reached another turn in my life, recognizing that my work at the Institute was in need of a new direction and that my spiritual life had become too predictable. Ruth and I took up the challenge to move to Indiana to assist in the renewal of a century-old conference and retreat center. Once again, I have received much more than I could have known how to ask for, both in challenges and rewards. Now on a weekly basis, I am privileged to share this life-work I discovered.

The challenges have pushed me beyond the spiritual resources I had discovered in those early years of awakening to discover a yet deeper ground of divine grace.

Do I still long for constant awareness of God? Yes. Yet, now I also understand more fully the unfolding nature of this development. God works on us, as Meister Eckhart expressed: "bit by bit." No, I cannot say that I have arrived at the enlightened awareness of God's constant presence. But I can say that I now know for sure that it is not a vain promise, but a potentiality worth devoting one's life toward. In striving toward it, I have learned also a profound compassion for the struggle we each bring to authentic spiritual life. This quest for God exists in the experience of the mystics of the ages. It exists sometimes in my own awareness. It is not an idle wish to seek to fill our noisy minds with the silent conviction of divine guidance. The way is not easy, but the quest is the most significant we can undertake.

I am most grateful to Timothy and Nancy Crouch of OSL Publications for bringing forth this new edition of *Christian Meditation and Inner Healing*. I also express my profound appreciation for the encouragement through the years toward all of my publishing endeavors by John White, literary agent. Finally, what a privilege it has been and continues to be to share the inner way with so many people.

Deo gratias!

Oakwood Spiritual Life Center
Syracuse, Indiana
January, 2000

CHAPTER ONE

A New Heaven and a New Earth: A New Mind and a New Body

A phone rings in my sleep. Heartbeat doubles its pace. I stumble out of bed in the darkness, look but cannot see the clock to tell what time it is. A voice out of the receiver at my ear speaks: "I'm going to kill myself. I have all the preparations made; the letters written; the children are away. Will you pray for me?"

My voice is calm, inside I am terror-struck. What can I do, what can I say? This time I know it is not a gesture, but a carefully thought out plan. Keep talking. . . a few more minutes. . . My God! . . .

At last a neighbor breaks in. A life is saved. But the terror remains in my heart.

The voice on the other end of the telephone has been my voice and it has been yours; perhaps not as desperate, perhaps not as despairing; but, we have all heard such reverberations in our hearts. Many of us are face to face with such despair in our daily work with individuals and social systems that are struggling for authentic life. How do we remain sensitive to the pain of the human struggle and not retreat into despair?

This is a book about Christian meditation. It is a book of methods that enable us to probe that question in our inner and outer worlds. Our companions in this search for a human life of hope range from St. Paul to St. Bonaventure, Meister Eckhart, St. Teresa of Avila, the practitioners of Eastern Orthodox *hesychasm*, and the anonymous author of *The Cloud of Unknowing*. We are looking for the way of actualizing the promised hope of Christianity into our hearts and minds, our motivations and daily discernments. We are

1

seeking a contemporary version of the mystic way: the way of dedication to God that works a transformation of the personality into Christ's loving presence. We are seeking the inspiration of a victorious Christ, who has overcome the world's despair and death and who has invited us into "abundant life." We seek such life or "eternal life-force" not merely as an idea to hold fast to, but as an actualized experience in our hearts, as a way of hopeful life.

The way toward this eternal-life-force awareness has been trod by many earnest people of all religious traditions. They have universally pointed to the necessity of cultivating a certain kind of inner awareness or meditative attention to ourselves in order to heal our inner strife and claim the inner peace that is promised.

This book will explore the distinctive features of Christian meditation and inner healing. We will begin by looking at the nature of Christian hope, especially as derived in the writings of St. Paul. It is my contention that the contemporary problem for human existence is not the question that has so dominated Christian theology in the past. That old question was the question of guilt: How can sin be redeemed? The contemporary question goes more deeply into existential suffering: How can we hope in a world of paradox and suffering? How can we envision a future in a world threatened by nuclear and ecological extinction? The question of hope must first be answered before we can begin to chart our lives toward the other questions of existence: guilt, authenticity, and service.

There is an emerging new paradigm of human life, emerging in spite of all the despairing signs of planetary crisis. That emerging paradigm looks to the possibility of humanity taking responsibility for its actions and acting in concert with divine hope for the redemption of individual and planetary suffering. This paradigm is rooted in the resurrection hope: new life is always springing from old; death is not the final answer; God is eternally recreating and renewing earthly existence. The paramount issue for us individually is how to develop an awareness of that eternally recreating/renewing divine presence.

Throughout Christian history, there have been individuals who have sought to claim this most essential Christianity. They have learned to pray, they have learned to wrestle with their inner struggles, and they have learned to listen for a divine center within themselves. We will explore the ways of inner listening that these individuals have discovered.

2

My primary purpose in writing this book is to describe Christian meditation practices in a way that combines historical practices with contemporary psychological awareness. From time to time, I will refer to a newly emerging psychology called transpersonal psychology. The task of this field is to develop a psychology that integrates the wisdom of spiritual traditions with current developments in Western psychology. I have thus undertaken more than the description of prayer practices. I have also sought to lay the foundation for the psychological understanding that allows us to make sense of our inner experiences in prayer and meditation. In addition, I have sought to lay a clear biblical foundation to this work.

Because of these multiple tasks, it may be helpful to the reader to begin where your interests are most keen, rather than necessarily with the first chapter. A brief summary of chapters is given to assist you in finding your interests.

The remainder of chapter 1 is devoted to the biblical foundation for Christian meditation and a further discussion of the theme of hope as a basis for Christian meditation work. Chapter 2 discusses a transpersonal model of consciousness and speaks of the recovery of the notion of soul as a principle for our inner work. Chapter 3 describes a general view of meditation practices and sets the context of Christian meditation within the broader field of the psychology of meditation. Chapters 4 through 7 are devoted to Christian meditation practices, specifically, meditation on God in creation, scriptural meditation, the Jesus Prayer, and Centering Prayer. Chapter 8 gives guidance for undertaking a regular meditation practice, discusses the possibilities of working within a group context, and speaks of the possibility of cultivating an attitude of contemplative discernment.

May the work of contemplative prayer bring you to the fullness of life for which you hope. May you discover the richness of your own interior wellspring of divine life.

DISCOVERING THE CELEBRATIVE CENTER

How do we characterize the hope of the Christian quest? How do we begin to actualize the experience of this essential Christianity in our hearts and minds? How do we claim the mystic vision of dwelling in the constant awareness of God?

A number of years ago, before I discovered the wealth of literature on inner-life development, I struggled to personalize this vision of life within divine presence. What characterizes the state of awareness that arises from the mystic vision? How could you describe it in a bodily felt way? How would you speak of the center of health and hope within us that can be remembered, that can be touched from time to time?

As I struggled to put that concept into a feeling quality, the term "celebrative center" came to mind. I described the "place," which of course is not a place but a state of body and mind awareness, as the celebrative center within me.

Through the years, as I have explored many methods of meditation, psychotherapy, and body therapies, the term "celebrative center" has continued to have meaning. I think of it now as a point of equilibrium, which of course is not a point, but a moment in which concerns of mind, spirit, and body are balanced. Yet the term "celebrative center" also has a dynamism of its own, pointing to the divine urge within us that leads us toward wholeness.

Others have described this state of being in other metaphors. St. Teresa of Avila, writing in the sixteenth century, described the inner world as an interior castle (Judy, 1996, Kavanaugh and Rodriguez 1980). The same dynamism is in St. Teresa's description. The center point was God enthroned upon the heart in radiant splendor. God is radiating outward to bring wholeness to all the divergent parts of the person.

This divine center, this center of light and life within us, whether we locate it in a special place like the heart, or in all the energies of the body and soul, is a metaphor and an experience of being centered, if for only a moment, in eternity. Within our bodies, we are constantly experiencing creation. We are told that every seven years the cells of our body have completely renewed. Furthermore, within our unconscious memory, we each have registered the experience of being created physically from conception to birth. The mystery of creation is not something alien to us; it is an ever-present reality. To speak of a "celebrative center" or of the divine dwelling in our hearts in radiance is to try to put words to the awesome potentiality for renewal that is the life-giving source always with and within us.

The first thing we learn about God in the Judeo-Christian Scriptures is that God creates. God's very essence is to be creating. Meister Eckhart in the fourteenth century stated God's essence in this way: "What does God do all day long? God gives birth. From all eternity God lies on a maternity bed giving birth" (Fox 1983, 220). In Genesis the first words of Scripture are "in the beginning, God was creating" (1:1).

To be in touch with the celebrative center is to allow our minds, bodies, and emotions to reconnect with the center of divine creative energy. Abiding perpetually in that presence is what Jesus means by living life reborn in the Spirit (John 3). And such life in the Spirit for Jesus was filled with the unexpected, filled with opportunities for new creation, filled with what he called life eternal.

Such life at the celebrative/creative center leads to a new mind and a new body. As we explore the potentials of inner healing through Christian meditation, we are invited by the essential teachings of Jesus as well as the other writings of Scripture to be open to radical possibility. New life does come to us. Minds are changed. Bodies are released from stresses and, in some cases, disease. Hearts are cleansed of hurts and bitterness.

Another way of describing the new life we seek is to speak of a grace-full or graceful life. The graceful life is one in which we have learned repeatedly to trust the unfolding creative spirit in our lives. We have learned to let go of a way of being when the time has come to release. We have learned to hear the call of the new wind of the Spirit when the new is beckoning. We are intentionally living in harmony with the many levels of community to which we relate. We have made peace with our passions and learned to forgive. Such graceful life is life in Christ and life brought to wholeness through Christ.

Our meditation practice will bring us into direct relationship with our minds and bodies. We will explore the habits of thought that have been largely unconscious, and yet motivate us and often drive our lives. We will be brought into contact with the emotional patterns that dominate our relationships. We will explore the places of holding tension within our bodies. And we will come into direct relationship with the divine that already resides within us and that is seeking to motivate us toward health and toward meaningful service within the world community. In short, the work of meditation is a transformative work. There are also pitfalls along the way. These, too, we will explore. Yet the road we travel in a serious inner journey is the journey toward a new mind and a new body, a being awakening to divine possibility and divine hope.

Spirit calls to our spirits. There is often a compelling urge to discover more of life, to find new meaning and purpose. At such times beginning a regular meditation practice may be very appropriate. In her description of the deepening of spiritual life, St. Teresa of Avila speaks of a time when

5

it is necessary to undertake a personal meditative prayer practice if we are not to stagnate. Before then she indicates that we are well nourished spiritually with "external" means: inspiring sermons, books, and conversations. She also calls life's trials one of these external means. When we are in trouble we reach out to God. But, she says, there comes a time when we must enter our own interior world and find God there if we are to move forward spiritually (Kavanaugh and Rodriguez 1980, 298). I suspect that the spiritual hunger rampant in the developed world fits her description well. We are accustomed to turning our attention outwardly. Yet we yearn for more clarity of meaning in our lives. And as we learn increasingly about the crises facing our world, we are bewildered with choices for placing our energy and resources in a meaningful way. We are drawn to look within both for our own personal healing and for discernment of appropriate service within the world. We are compelled to discover the divine source in a direct way, and to gain clarity and regeneration for daily living.

We are compelled to look for a new mind and a new body, enlivened by divine creativity. We yearn to live from the celebrative/creative center.

THE BIRTH OF HOPE

"The Realm of God is at hand."

Jesus proclaimed this mystic vision. "The Realm of God is at hand." The day of peace, the day of reconciliation is here. There is no need to look further or to await further revelation. Now is the "day of the Lord."

The early church wrestled with the contradiction between this proclamation and the obvious lack of peace, reconciliation, and loving attitudes within the world. The world did not reflect this "day of the Lord." The world exhibited the way of conflict and destruction. The world in which Christianity was born was a world in chaos. It was the era of the latter days of the Roman empire. It was a time when the Temple in Israel was destroyed. It was a time of immense external change. It was a time of internal change, when a new mind was being forged in the inner crucible of the human soul.

Jesus gave us the vision for our age, a seemingly contradictory and inexplicable statement that provides the catalyst for our personal and social hope: God's Realm is at hand, the day of the Lord is here.

It is my view that the mystic hope is to embody this vision, to live experientially in its promise. We are forever dissatisfied with the Christian message until we claim this message for ourselves and seek to realize it in our day-to-day existence.

As St. Paul wrestled with the seeming contradiction of this promise of Jesus, he spoke of it as the paradox of hope. For Paul, hope was born into human consciousness with Jesus. And it is a hope that pertains to both individuals and social orders, indeed to everything in creation. "Up to the present, we know, the whole created universe groans in all its parts as if in the pangs of childbirth. Not only so but even we, to whom the Spirit is given as firstfruits of the harvest to come, are groaning inwardly while we wait for God to make us his sons [and daughters] and set our whole body free. For we have been saved, though only in hope" (Romans 8:22-24, NEB). It is very important that we understand the radical nature of hope for Paul, for it lays the groundwork for the Christian life as expressed throughout the Christian era. It is also at the heart of the mystical quest and the work of Christian meditation and inner healing.

This hope for Paul is at the heart of human longing and human healing. Do we dare to hope so fully? Is it possible for our whole body to be set free? Our primal wound is that we do not live consciously moment to moment with divine awareness and guidance. Sin is the name Paul gave to that primal wound. Sin, for Paul, is the separation from God within us that plagues us and fills us with despair. It is the split from which human society suffers so greatly. Hope for Paul is born in the realization that this primal wound has been overcome in Jesus and therefore is being overcome in every other human being and in every other created entity.

Paul's radical hope is born of a mystical awakening. He had received a direct vision of Christ in his famous encounter on the road to Damascus. Such direct encounters with the wholeness of life, whether dramatic like Paul's or more subtle, are also the birth of hope in each of us. We each contain within ourselves the possibility for such direct knowing, for such moments of clarity of life purpose. In such moments, we directly experience the "day of the Lord." "The Realm of God" is fully present. Hope has been born that we may live every moment in such reconciling peace and love. Hope has been born and now seeks to penetrate every fiber of our beings and every moment of our lives. The celebrative/creative center has awakened.

Paul elucidated this life of contradictory hope in two primary arenas: the inner struggles of the individual and the struggles of communities to live together in harmony. His language is compelling, and it has been grossly misunderstood. I think it is no accident that Paul used the language of the body to seek to make his points. Unfortunately, his very language of the body has through time taken on connotations opposite from his original intentions. However, as we understand his intention more fully, I think we begin to see the parallels to current psychological thinking.

The epitome of human hope for Paul is that God will "set our whole body free." He also refers to the inward groaning of all creation, as if in the pangs of childbirth. His language is graphic and physically oriented. The whole creation intensely feels the distortions of sin. It is no great leap from Paul's language to the language of contemporary ecologists who now speak of the earth as a living organism threatened by the overload of human life. Nor is his language too distant from current thinking regarding the integration of mind and body. According to many practitioners of psychophysical integration, areas of chronic pain and discomfort in the body are related to psychological distress. Paul's language of the body expresses very well the hope of such contemporary practitioners: that the whole body will be set free. By this phrase, such therapists now mean that the basic wounds of an individual have been identified and that their emotional burden has been released. A freer mental attitude and a freer feeling within one's body result from such release.

While Paul does not necessarily envision such a release from the constrictions within the body, he was no stranger to the phenomenon of physical healing. His language constantly points to the possibility of the transformation of our deepest inner natures and the potential for charting new life directions through Christ's awakened creative presence.

Paul's imagery of the body's struggle reveals a tension among interior motivations. And herein lies one of the most misunderstood of his concepts. For Paul, the "flesh" or the "lower nature" means a set of attitudes that are life-destructive. He outlines these in Galatians: "fornication, impurity, and indecency; idolatry and sorcery; quarrels, a contentious temper, envy, fits of rage, selfish ambitions, party intrigues, and jealousies; drinking bouts, orgies, and the like" (5:20, NEB). Life in the flesh or lower nature is contrasted with life in the Spirit: "the harvest of the Spirit is love, joy, peace, patience, kindness, goodness, fidelity, gentleness, and self-control" (5:22, NEB). Paul speaks of the lower nature being "crucified" with Christ Jesus. Thus the "flesh" or the lower nature does not mean the whole "body" for Paul. It rather means being enslaved to one's passions and addictive behaviors without regard to social consequence. In short, it means being victimized by our own natures rather than awakening the compassionate spirit and allowing it to pervade our bodies. For something to be crucified for Paul means that one is truly "dead" to it, that is, it has ceased to be a problem. The problem has been transformed. In his description of the crucifixion of the lower nature, we see Paul's radical hope for human transformation, a transformation of motivation and inner emotional states.

In later Christian writing, the method for healing this deep interior wound is described in this equally radical statement: "the contemplative work of love by itself will eventually heal you of all the roots of sin" (Johnston 1973, 64). We hear in this statement from the fourteenth-century writing, *The Cloud of Unknowing*, the same audacious hope expressed by Paul. Human nature can be redeemed. The primal wound can be healed. There is a possibility of living our lives every moment in the awareness of the Realm of God. The quest for this interior transformation has been the task of the Christian mystical tradition. It is a quest not merely for the change of behavior, but for the change of interior motivations. It is the quest for a transformation of human nature toward the expression of divine compassion to the extent that the individual experiences an interior reconciliation, an interior peace, an interior certainty of divine presence and radiant life. This quest for such interior transformation will form the basis of our work in Christian meditation.

The context for such inner transformation is life in relationship with other people and creatures. Christian life concerns itself not only with interior transformation, but also with exterior transformation, the transformation of the primal wound within communities and within all creation. To this end, Paul's language of the body is also very revealing. He speaks of communities as bodies. The church for Paul is the "body of Christ." What an intriguing concept. The church is the body of the resurrected Christ in any historical era. The resurrected Christ is Spirit, but continues to act in historical time through the body of those who call themselves by his name. The hope awakened by Jesus continues to work on human society and culture, on nations and creation. But Christ needs our bodies, our lives of flesh and blood and time and place to actualize the new vision of creation.

The language of the body for a community anticipates systems theories of organizational behavior. We, in any community, are literally one flesh with each other. We act as an organism. And the individual sufferings of interior motivations become magnified when placed in the context of community. For an individual to possess a streak of sadistic behavior, if actualized, will injure a few people in his or her lifetime. For a society systematically to brutalize one faction within it injures whole races. The primal wounds of individuals become the corporate sins of racism, institutionalized injustice, and systematic blindness to human and environmental suffering. All this Paul's language of the body anticipates when he states: "For Christ is like a single body with its many limbs and organs, which many as they are, together make up one body. For indeed we were all brought into one body by baptism, in the one Spirit, whether we are Jews or Greeks, whether slaves or free [persons], and that one Holy Spirit was poured out for all of us to drink" (1 Corinthians 12:12-13, NEB).

We may readily note the theme of hope raised now to the social level. This new community Paul described overcomes the divisions of enmity within a society. In his time these were the division between Jew and Gentile, and certainly as radical, the division between slaves and free people. What are the current divisions within human society? Where are the signs of the collective body of humanity understanding itself to be true partners one with another? *There* we find the body of Christ. And we must acknowledge that the formal church may have become an agent of division as well as an agent of incorporation and social transformation.

Paul uses the language of the body to point to the importance of each individual to the functioning of the whole. What would be a body without a head or without feet, he asks. How can you say that one part is more important than another? Here Paul brings forward in a graphic way the fundamental teaching of Jesus of respect for neighbor and of honoring the "least among you."

The most fundamental issues of interior pain of the individual are also issues of social life. The issues of motivation that Paul addresses as ways of "flesh" or "Spirit" are attitudes of social interaction. The human heart is social in nature. When we are wrestling with our most difficult issues of motivation or of interior conflict, we are wrestling with issues of relationship, past, present, or future. As we explore the themes of inner healing through Christian meditation, this principle will guide us. We will amplify it substantially. At this point, however, we can merely say that Christian tradition holds the arena of social interaction before us to be addressed both within ourselves in our inner conflicts and outside ourselves in the concern for the nature of communities themselves. Are communities moving toward the wholeness and inclusiveness envisioned by Paul's "body of Christ" or do they promote diminution of the human spirit?

The interpenetration of the interior and the exterior worlds are brought into perspective in two other key concepts of Judeo-Christian teaching. The concept of *shalom* from Hebrew thought and the concept of *hesychasm* from the Eastern Orthodox tradition of Christianity point us in the same direction: the actualization of the Realm of God as a present reality. *Shalom* means peace, but it means peace in a very particular way. It does not mean my peace at the cost of your suffering. It means all things in such right relationship that peace reigns. It is like Paul's body of Christ in which all parts function effectively and respect all other parts. It is the opposite of opportunistic use of one another for gain. *Shalom* does not prevail unless attention is given to the least within a society. *Shalom* guided the Hebrew prophets to speak against the garnering of wealth for a privileged few at the expense of the weak. It prompted the concern for the widowed and orphaned within that culture. At its best *shalom* was actualized in the tradition of jubilee, in which periodically all debts were forgiven, all prisoners released, all society given a fresh start. *Shalom* reigns on the Sabbath, when individuals rest from their labors and simply experience the renewing grace of God.

The concept of *hesychasm* from Eastern Orthodox tradition personalizes *shalom*. *Hesychasm* means tranquility or peace, but not in a way that isolates the individual from the social context. The term was used to describe the aim of practitioners of inner prayer. *Hesychasm* is not achieved in isolation from one's concerns of relationship. *Hesychasm* conveys a spirit of inner and outward tranquility. That is, one is in right relationship both to the inner world and to the outer world, so that the kingdom of peace is lived moment to moment, day to day, year after year.

Is that not what we each long for? Do we not long to live in this world of change in a spirit of actualized peace? And do we not long to know that our own efforts at peacemaking within ourselves and within our small arenas of responsibility contribute toward the creation of *shalom* within the world community? The spirit of contemplative love we will cultivate bridges these inward and outward concerns.

Those are the issues that arise in any meaningful spiritual life. Those are the issues that Christian meditation assists us to address.

A NEW HEAVEN AND A NEW EARTH

The imagery of the Revelation of John draws us toward the inexorable hope of a new creation enlivened by *shalom*. John of Patmos speaks of a new heaven and a new earth. His vision is the completion of the creation groaning in the travail of childbirth of which Paul speaks. John's vision takes us forward in time and forward in hope to envision the cooperation of earth and heaven in a new way.

> Then I saw a new heaven and a new earth, for the first heaven and the first earth had vanished, and there was no longer any sea. I saw the holy city, new Jerusalem, coming down out of heaven from God, made ready like a bride adorned for her husband. I heard a loud voice proclaiming from the throne: "Now at last God has his dwelling among men [and women]! He will dwell among them and they shall be his people, and God himself will be with them. He will wipe every tear from their eyes; there shall be an end to death, and to mourning and crying and pain; for the old order has passed away!" (Revelation 21:1-4, NEB)

There is no Temple in John's new Jerusalem, "for its temple was the sovereign Lord God and the Lamb" (21:23). Furthermore the earth is restored to bounty and the servants of God see him "face to face, and bear his name on their foreheads" (22:3).

Here the promise of the Realm of God is most graphically presented. The curses of the Fall of Eden are removed. The Tree of Life is found.

> Then he showed me the river of the water of life, sparkling like crystal, flowing from the throne of God and of the Lamb down the middle of the city's street. On either side of the river stood a tree of life, which yields twelve crops of fruit, one for each month of the year; the leaves of the trees serve for the healing of the nations. Every accursed thing shall disappear. (22:1-2)

Well, what does all this mysterious imagery have to do with the healing of you and me and of our twenty-first-century earth? I think it points precisely to our present age with its potential for healing.

The new heaven and the new earth are *now* to be actualized. We note that the new city comes forth from heaven, which in mythic metaphor would mean from the realm of ideas. The new city must be birthed from an awakened human spirit in concert with the divine Spirit. The new city is also inhabited by people who now see God face to face. There is no Temple, because the Temple is an intermediary place. And now the people are able to relate one to one with God. Furthermore the curse of Cain is removed. God's name is written upon their foreheads. Here we have the imagery of the radiance associated with divine presence and with the awakening of the intuitive "third eye," described in other mystical traditions. In the book of Genesis, Cain, the brother of us all, has been sent off wandering the earth in exile because he slew his brother Abel. God placed a mark on his forehead so that he would not be slain. But Cain is also "marked" eternally for his sin. Here in the new city the mark of sin is healed by the mark of divine inspiration, and radiance shows forth from every child of God.

In this new heaven and new earth there is bounty enough for all the creatures. The Tree of Life gives forth its fruit in due season. I suggest this tree is another image for the hope that eternally motivates us to create the world toward a wholeness of life in which there is food enough for all and in which there is a lessening of disease and suffering. And it is a new heaven and a new earth when these achievements spring forth from the combined minds of earnest human beings and the divine source.

To dwell in the vision of this new reality is to be inspired to work and suffer and struggle for it to be actualized. Thus we always pray, "Thy kingdom come, Thy will be done on earth, as it is in heaven." Such is the hope that will not die in the human heart, regardless of all the evidence of the victories of destruction. Such eternal presence does this hope have that it is called divine.

Now, to incorporate that hope, to embody that hope, to allow it to penetrate to the very core of our being so that we are that hope is the essence of Christian transformation. To live unwaveringly in the presence of such hope is to dwell in contemplative love.

John of Patmos takes the birth of the hope of which Paul speaks and makes it absolutely clear that this hope is to penetrate into the structures of physical and social life. No arena is to be left untouched by it. The creation is to be redeemed from its suffering.

The essential challenge of our faith stance is whether we will allow ourselves to be captivated by this radical hope and submit ourselves into the service of the transformation of ourselves and our world. Service of God means such transformative service to the world and to the ongoing process of the conversion of our inner beings toward unswerving hope.

It happens that I originally wrote these words on December 7, 1988, the anniversary of Pearl Harbor and the day that then General Secretary Mikhail Gorbachev addressed the United Nations General Assembly. His address signaled the end of the Cold War. Never in my imagination would I have dreamed the possibility of such a cessation of hostilities in my lifetime. Yet on December 7, 1988, we began to dream of that possibility. The vision of John of Patmos almost two thousand years ago encourages us to dream the dream of actualized hope in human society. His dream is of the universal lessening of human suffering, of disease and death, of crying and mourning: the old order, he says, has passed away!

WHOLENESS AND HOLINESS

When we live with our awareness attuned to this divine hope for individuals and societies, an ongoing transformation occurs within our own beings. A much neglected doctrine of the church has spoken of this transforming relationship to the divine. That is the doctrine of *sanctification*. The word comes from the Latin word meaning holy. Sanctification describes the lifelong process of growth into God. The contemporary description of this process in Roman Catholic theology is *divinization*: the process of being wholly made over into the divine. These words of doctrine are the attempt to describe the transformative renewal that comes from contact with the divine source of creative energy. When we are living in constant awareness of the divine source our minds, hearts, and bodies are available for constant renewal. Ultimately our motivations become centered in divine compassion and hope. St. Teresa spoke of the alignment of wills. The individual human will becomes one with the divine will. However we speak of this divine/human union, it is awesome to consider. Yet, it has indeed been considered and proclaimed throughout Christian history.

Many descriptions have been attempted. The *hesychasts* of Eastern Orthodoxy have practiced a form of devotional prayer to Jesus called the Jesus Prayer, which takes one into union with God through union with Jesus. Meister Eckhart spoke of becoming so present to our own being that finally we experience our "is-ness" and God's "is-ness" as one "is-ness," in which there is neither God nor ourselves but one quality of "being-ness." "I advise you to let your

14

own 'being you' sink into and flow away into God's 'being God.' Then your 'you' and God's 'his' will become so completely one 'my' that you will eternally know with him his changeless existence and his nameless nothingness" (Fox 1980, 179). St. Teresa of Avila spoke of a marriage of the individual with God culminating in a state of complete day-to-day activity (Kavanaugh and Rodriguez 1980, 434). John Wesley spoke of the perfection of love, in which the individual was so transformed that she or he might find "purity of intention, . . . the renewal of the heart in the whole image of God" (Sugden 1921, 1968, 148). Dante criticized the classical world of ancient Rome and Greece for a failure of its philosophers to envision ecstasy, life lived in direct communion with the "primal love" of the divine. St. Bonaventure spoke of "the soul's journey into God," in which he explored all aspects of human personality and creation as reflections of the "footprints" or "vestiges" of God, until one was finally led into ecstatic contemplation of God directly.

When we explore models of inner-life development, we find descriptions of a period of dislocation, as the inner world is awakening. A period of intense purification follows, as all aspects of personal motivations, emotional responses, and mental attitudes are explored. Finally, a new point of equilibrium emerges as the new mind and body emerge, now rooted joyously in God. The soul's journey into God is a journey into wholeness. One of the major contributions of the psychological understanding of our time is that we must make peace with our inner drives and urges, with our passions and emotional complexes.

There are writings within the Christian life that create great internal strife. There has been a tendency to deny the body and the emotions a proper place in the "new mind and new body" of the transformed being. It is my belief, well supported by much of the contemplative literature, that such an approach creates further alienation within our psyches and drives us away from peace rather than toward it. We will explore in the next chapter a model of the human being that takes into account our challenges as well as our light. We will begin exploring the process of holiness as a process of wholeness. We will look toward the origins and the potentials for healing our many inner wounds, and we will explore the recovery of the idea of soul as our guiding principle.

In the chapters that will follow we will explore the methods of Christian meditation: meditating on God in creation, meditation on Scripture, the Jesus Prayer, and Centering Prayer. A final chapter will give guidance in undertaking a meaningful meditation practice.

CHAPTER TWO

Recovering the Soul

We live in an age that has lost touch with the ways of the soul. Native cultures have a term called soul-loss, which is the most serious illness possible. Soul-loss means that one's essential nature has somehow been separated from one's day-to-day existence. How fascinating that in twentieth-century Western culture the term "soul" should have lost its meaning. We may tentatively speak of our souls, but we have lost a meaningful definition within our culture. In the last twenty years, Western culture has begun the first steps toward recovering its understanding of soul.

Jacob Needleman, in his stimulating book *Lost Christianity*, published in 1980, speaks of this loss of definition for the soul. "We are seeking to bring back the symbolic power of the idea of the soul, to recover it as a guide to the search for ourselves, our lost selves" (1980, 189). Needleman goes on to describe the process of creating our souls. He says that one of the problems of Christianity is that it has not been clear enough regarding the developmental process of the soul. "It is rare that any Christian writer ever explicitly states that man has a soul only in potential" (ibid., 213). Needleman then describes the need to understand that work is required to develop the potentiality of soul. For this process, he speaks of the necessity of undertaking the esoteric practices of spiritual traditions, those practices that show us how to be with our own inner experience. Our task is to develop *"intermediate man [and woman]*, who alone in the cosmic scheme can care for, or harmonize, or relate all the Forces of creation" (ibid., 181).

Do we understand the place of humankind to be in this intermediary position, relating to all the forces of creation? Do we understand ourselves individually to be capable of such relationship? Such has historically been understood as the capability of the human soul. Recall the "great chain of being" of medieval philosophy. Every creature from the tiniest to God had a place. Humankind had an exalted place and was the only one of all the creatures who could relate to all the others. *The Cloud of Unknowing* states this understanding:

> Beneath you and external to you lies the entire created universe. Yes, even the sun, the moon, and the stars. They are fixed above you splendid in the firmament, yet they cannot compare to your exalted dignity as a human being.... As [a person] you are related to everything in creation through the medium of your faculties. If you understand all this about the hierarchy of creation and your own nature and place in it, you will have some criteria for evaluating the importance of each of your relationships. (Johnston 1973, 129)

The capacities of the soul were understood to be grand: relating to all creatures and to God, to the departed "souls of the just," as well as angels and the mystical presence of Christ. The human faculties mentioned here are mind (the capacity for integrating all interior realities), reason, will, imagination, and feeling. The senses are another of the faculties not explicitly mentioned in *The Cloud of Unknowing*, but clearly mentioned in other medieval texts, in particular St. Bonaventure's *The Soul's Journey into God*. Through these faculties the soul relates to all that is. How developed is our capacity for imagination, for feeling, for reason, for the exercise of will, for acuity of the senses? Those themes we will explore in our practice of Christian meditation. For now the question I raise is whether we have a notion of the soul-in-potential, as capable of expanding into the intermediate being, of which Needleman speaks.

I suggest that one of the major problems of contemporary life is that we have lost this exalted notion of the human soul. And therein lies the cornerstone of our soul-loss. There is a paradox of enormous power at work here. If we do not think highly enough of ourselves as human beings then we do not consider the enormous consequences of our actions. We see that fact most dramatically at work in the ecological crisis. Because we have not understood the interdependence of all things, we have not taken our individual roles in producing exhaust emissions and chlorofluorocarbons seriously. Each of us matters. The facts are now inescapable. Humankind has entered into a role of co-creation with the forces of earth. We hold the fate of species in our hands. We might read these problems as a result of humankind assuming too exalted a role in the scheme of nature. To be sure there is a problem of appropriate humility. But I suggest the real problem is that humanity does not think highly enough of itself, does not really accept its role as the intermediary force between creation and divine inspiration, does not acknowledge its awesome power of destruction. We need to recover the notion of soul as individuals and as a species. We are interrelating to all that is. We must bring those relationships to consciousness. And we must learn to use our power for good. We must learn to stand "in relationship to both time and eternity" (Needleman 1980,180).

Such a stance requires the forging of soul within ourselves. Needleman calls us to the hard work of living in the "psychological pain of contradiction.... When man is in question, he is actually in between the higher and the lower in himself" (ibid., 176). I suggest that this is the same method used by Jesus in his hard sayings on discipleship. He constantly called for decisions, for decisions to which there were not easy answers. And he himself exhibited the willingness to suffer with hard choices. Such is the work of the soul. Needleman calls it "living the question." We actually place ourselves willingly in the midst of the yet unsolved struggles, the contradictions, the open-ended places, and take our responsibility as the intermediary force we can be, integrating the opposing forces within ourselves and about us. Soul work is difficult.

Through the living of these contradictions, suffering through to reconciliations, we do two simultaneous works. On the one hand we solve problems. We offer our own creativity to the solution of the problem that presents itself. And second, and equally important, we become more and more conscious of our own capacities. Each time we enter this crucible of creativity, we learn a bit more about our "faculties:" we expand our capacity for feeling, for reason, for sensory perception, for imagination, and for the acts of will. We must do this soul-work of becoming more conscious of our capacities as humankind or we will surely perish and take the earth with us. That is the contemporary context for our spiritual growth. We cannot escape it. For this reason, Ken Wilber, one of the critical thinkers of our time, has called "a new categorical imperative" of our age to be the willingness of us individually to undertake a meditative or contemplative practice (1981b, 321). Carl Jung spoke of the critical necessity of our becoming conscious of the forces at work within us (1969, 9-I, §487). Such is the work of the soul.

DEVELOPING SOUL

How would we begin to develop the capacities of the soul? James Hillman has written provocatively on the nature of the soul in his book *Re-Visioning Psychology* (1975). Hillman speaks from the perspective of psychology and the need within the field of psychology to recover the depth dimension of the human being contained in the notion of soul. He calls the task of human life to be *soul-making*. The term is derived from the Romantic poets and is used by John Keats. Similar notions are found in the writings of William Blake. Keats writes: "Call the world if you please, 'The vale of Soul-making.' Then you will find out the use of the world..." (ix). He continues, "From this perspective the human adventure is a wandering through the vale of the world for the sake of making soul. Our life is psychological, and the purpose of life is to make psyche of it, to find connections between life and soul" (ix). By soul, he means a "viewpoint" or a "perspective," the ability to create a "reflective moment" between perception and action. "Soul-making means differentiating this middle ground" (x). In Hillman's description, we find parallels to Needleman's question as the formulating principle of soul. When we allow ourselves the viewpoint to stand in between perception and response and also in between all the forces of the universe, we have entered the realm of the soul.

While Hillman refers to the process of developing soul as "soul-making," I prefer the term "ensouling." Soul-making implies too much hubris for my taste. We do not make our souls; we discover them. Yet it is hard work to undertake this process of discovery. The term "ensouling" speaks to the simultaneous dynamic of effort and receptivity.

The language of ensouling is not the language of reason. It is instead the language of fantasy, metaphor, poetry. "By *soul*, I mean the imaginative possibility of our natures, the experiencing through reflective speculation, dream, image and *fantasy* — that mode which recognizes all realities as primarily symbolic or metaphorical" (ibid., x). Hillman identifies the soul with imagination. He draws our attention to the meaning of the Greek word for soul, *psyche*, which is also the name of the beautiful woman in the story of Eros and Psyche. The word also means night-moth or butterfly. The images give the connotation of the feminine, of the night, and of dreams. "Soul is imagination, a cavernous treasury — to use an image from St. Augustine — a confusion and richness, both" (ibid., 68-69). Hillman criti-

19

cizes Christianity for bringing suspicion to the realm of fantasy and dreams. He suggests that the cavernous treasury of the soul has been increasingly limited by the Christian quest for purity, and then given a final blow with the rise of Cartesian empiricism and its exclusive emphasis on reason.

For Hillman, the Greek worldview with its use of gods and goddesses provided a rich context for the soul. The psychic powers were named in their unique characteristics. They were personified and called gods. Through this practice, the numinous forces beyond individual consciousness were given proper respect.

We need in our time to recover a language of the soul so that it can communicate with us. I suggest that this process is taking place in the arena of psychology, particularly that of Jungian and transpersonal psychology. In these psychologies, the place of dream, symbol, and metaphor is emphasized. It is understood that what we know consciously of ourselves is only the minimum of what we are, that beneath and behind our consciousness are unconscious forces of such compelling power that they were once described as gods or goddesses. The name in our age for these forces, a name given prominence by Jung, is archetypes.

The archetypes themselves are universal and transcend the images through which they speak. They are the great universal principles, such as the Father, Mother, Child, Sage, Hero, Warrior, Healer, Teacher, Laborer, Self, to name a few. Jung characterized the archetypes as the impersonal and universal structures upon which the individual psyche is built. Furthermore, he described these archetypal powers as having their own autonomous existence apart from our consciousness of them. When we are encountered by such an archetype, "it exerts a fascination, it enters into active opposition to the conscious mind, and may be said in the long run to mould the destinies of individuals by unconsciously influencing their thinking, feeling, and behaviour, even if this influence is not recognized until long afterwards" (Jung 1967, 5, §467). In the world of the Greeks and other similar mythological cultures, the archetypes were given personality and called the gods and goddesses.

Today we are left with only a remnant of this rich tapestry of the soul. Scripture has left in our conscious memory the direct encounters of divine energies: the angel Gabriel; the resurrected Christ; Mary, the Queen of Heaven. But by and large, we are left to discern our inner drives, struggles, and longings without recourse to divine intermediary figures of insight and wisdom. We are left on our own to struggle to discern the meaning of our boredoms, rages, and quiet desperations, which may, in fact, be the encounter of the numinous seeking to break through to us.

Many contemporary individuals will understand the powerful nature of the archetype of Father or Mother. As many people have delayed parenthood and come almost into middle age, what has been called the compelling urge of the biological clock to become parents I think is more accurately described as the call of the archetypes of parenthood to us. I speak here of my own personal experience. A compelling urge to be a parent was early present in me. Then I made peace with not being a father. In the mid-1980s the desire to be parent was so compelling for both my wife and myself that we yielded. And my life is now irrevocably changed. The Father has entered me, and I father two children. I will never again live apart from the Father archetype.

On one Christmas, while in the depths of longing for a child, we bought figures of Mary and the baby Jesus and brought them into our home as our central celebration of the season. At another time I found myself in a Catholic church praying to Joseph to bring us a child. These modes of expression, while alien to my own Protestant roots, accurately reflect the language of the soul. To personify the soul's longing in this way enables us to pray.

We live in an age when such expressions are somewhat alien. We have not been schooled in the soul's language of story, mythic image, and metaphor. It is no accident that at the close of his life Joseph Campbell's work on mythic image should spark the imagination of our culture. We are longing for the imagery, the mythic images, and the stories that help us make sense of our soul's journey. The rich tapestry of the world's mythologies speaks the language of the soul.

The language of the world's mythologies is the same language as our dream world. Our dreams each night help to make sense of our day's experiences and the movements of light and dark within us; they present our unfolding depth to us in the form of a story. It helps us greatly to understand our dreams if we treat them as mythic story. Conversely, it makes sense of mythology if we understand mythic story as the collective dream of its culture.

As we explore Christian meditation, we will find that there is one form in particular that relates to the awakening of imagination and the use of the Scripture story as our story. It is a tool that is very powerful for inner healing. It bridges the mythic worldview of Scripture into our own psychic experience. It opens the possibility of awakening

21

to authentic experiences of divine guidance. What we begin to find is that beneath the veneer of the rational mind is a realm of intuitive, imaginative potentiality, a wider range of human faculties that open for us the possibility for the inner healing of our memories and emotional suffering. As we imaginatively enter Scripture it helps us to personify the deep and mysterious longings within us and to make sense of the movements of the archetypal energies within our psyches.

AN INNER HEALING PROCESS

As we explore the kinds of inner healing that can be facilitated through Christian meditation, we will find a wide range of possibilities, including relief from physical and emotional distress. I will reserve our discussion of this theme for Chapter Five. But we will here explore an example of inner healing to enhance our understanding of the soul 's methods of communication and capacity for integration.

This situation occurred in a retreat in Christian meditation, that I facilitated in 1984. The subject was forty years old at the time. I will call him Tom. He is a Protestant minister who suffers from a chronic headache. The headache had been a part of his life for many years before this experience. When I spoke with him in 1988, his headache symptoms were still with him, yet he spoke of the profound impact of the following experience on his life and the unfolding healing of both the headache and the larger issues that emerged in the process described here.

Before our work in meditation and inner healing, he had explored the psychological implications of the headache in many ways. He had come to view the headache as a sign of the stress related to his relationship with his father and other male figures of authority.

One of the guided meditations in the retreat used imagination with Scripture in the style of the Ignatian exercises (Mottola 1964; Kelsey 1976). In the scriptural story, Jesus encounters the man at the pool of Bethsada who has been infirm for thirty years. Jesus asks the man if he wants to be healed and subsequently tells the man to take up his bed and walk (John 5). During this meditation, Tom experienced a profound sense of willingness to be healed of his headache. Christ was more vividly real in his inner world than ever before. The meditation ended with a long embrace between Tom and Christ, and the two of them walking off laughing together. All symptoms of the headache disappeared for three days.

The following week Tom invited further therapeutic work on the issue. The headache had returned. During the following session, I held various acupressure points on Tom's body to facilitate relaxation.

Dwight: We can return to the meditation experience or begin with the headache symptom.
Tom: I'd like to return to the meditation with you present.
D: [guidance back into the meditation and inquiry for relating what T is experiencing after a few minutes of silence in the meditation]
T: I'm with Jesus and we are sitting down embracing.
D: I feel like we have a co-therapy situation here, and I don't want to intrude on what you are experiencing with Jesus, but see if it feels appropriate for us to begin to explore the headache while you are being held by Christ.
T: Yes. That feels fine.
D: What we are wanting to do is to find out how the headache may be serving you, to begin to get acquainted, to start making friends. And it would help to have an image of some kind to talk with.
T: I've always thought of it as a witch or devil, not something I wanted to get to know but rather something to be cut out by a surgeon. I'm getting an image of a brown knotted muscle, but I'm not sure I want to get close enough to talk to it.
D: That's fine. You can take a surgical scalpel with you for protection. Can this muscle talk with you?
T: Yes. It has a mouth.
D: Ask it what it's doing for you, how is it serving you in some way?
T: [experienced difficulty at first in entering into conversation or imagining that there could be anything of benefit to come out of the very painful experience, then began to hear it comment on how long it had been trying to get through to him, to get its messages across]
D: Ask it for a memory of when it first started occurring.
T: [speaking as the muscle] I've been around a lot longer than you want to admit. [now speaking as himself] I see myself preaching [about fifteen years ago]. I'm trying so hard to do a good job. I want to be there, as a minister, but there are so many people

23

to try to please, so many expectations to come up to [mentions his supervising pastor]. I want to be Christ's messenger, but I'm doing it all with my head, with my carefully prepared manuscript. I feel very scared. Where are you, Jesus?

D: Was there ever a time when you felt Christ's presence as you preached, when you weren't afraid?

T: [slowly a memory comes in] There was once a time in Africa. I was the only white person in the village. They were having church and asked me to preach. And I had nothing prepared. I took up the flask of water I had brought with me, and talked about how I had no special message from Christ as a white man, that they had shown me Christ in their hospitality. That we were all drinking of the same water and they were Christ to me. Then I experienced that it wasn't me with my notes and my learning that was preaching. It was Christ in all of us [tears of relief and happiness].

D: I'd like to suggest that we go back to the other memory now and invite Christ to be there, too.

T: Yes. I see him coming down the aisle. He was there all the time, but I couldn't see him.

D: Invite him into that very spot where the headache lives, and now look out at the congregation through the eyes of Christ.

T: [more tears, more welcoming, and relief]

D: You have a wonderful new friend and can find lots of ways to get acquainted in the future. Now, as the session is closing, I'd like to invite you to go back to the old knotted muscle and exchange presents.

T: That seems really hard. I've hated you for so long. [silence] I was able to put down my scalpel, and the gift that came was a communion cup. And I gave the muscle a drink. It was so thirsty. I realized we were both thirsty. We both needed to drink the "living water." The muscle is not so brown, but redder. Its gift to me is to relax and let more blood flow through the veins.

T: [after coming out from deep imagery state] The muscle is my body, all the messages from the body that I've ignored, in order to live the way I thought I should.

24

In subsequent conversation, Tom reported having difficulty believing he was experiencing what he had experienced. The clarity and certainty of Christ's presence were not something that he had previously encountered. Nor did he have an intellectual understanding into which such experience could fit. Yet, he could not deny his experience of the healing and insight that it had brought. He also reported disbelief at the length of time that the session had involved, implying that he had experienced a realm of the psyche in which time is perceived differently than in waking consciousness.

IMPLICATIONS FOR ENSOULING

In this example of inner healing, there are three major characters who come into better communication with each other. One is Tom in his conscious understanding of himself or his ego. Tom's ego must be willing to open up to unexplored dimensions within himself before the inner healing process can begin. We notice Tom's surprise following the experience in the meditation, in which a new certainty of relationship with Christ was manifesting. We also notice that it is necessary for this ego to give full support to the possibility of change, as exhibited in the meditation when, at a deep level, Tom resolved to be willing to have the headache healed. We receive some clues as to the nature of Tom's ego and the dilemmas in which he is now struggling. "I want to be Christ's messenger, but I'm doing it all in my head, with my carefully prepared manuscript. I feel very scared. Where are you, Jesus?" Tom's ego is strongly identified with his rational function. Yet, there has been a stirring toward the mysteries represented by Christ and the religious dimension strong enough to bring him into the ministry. Tom wants to serve that which is beyond himself, but does not know how to experience that beyond.

This conflict manifests in the headache, the symptom of the body's unacknowledged fear, which is the second character in the story. Through the years, a constant battle is waged with the headache, and more and more it is seen as an enemy. Tom reported that it was a genuinely new idea to him that this symptom could have anything useful to tell him. Tom had created a relationship of enmity with it. So in our first encounter with it in the realm of myth, it appears as a witch or devil. After it takes the more physical form of the brown knotted muscle, Tom can approach it. Tom's ego fears are acknowledged, and he is given a scalpel as protection in approaching this muscle. We notice that Tom's fear indicates that the muscle is felt as more powerful than his ego. The years of conflict with the headache support this perception. It has not been within Tom's conscious power to overcome the headache. The headache is a message from one of those archetypes of which Jung speaks, "creating an active opposition to the conscious mind" (Jung 1967, 5, §467).

The muscle representing the headache contains a story within itself, including specific memories. In this case we recaptured two memories, one related to the presence of the headache, one related to the presence of Christ. The muscle has created its own story. A part of our task in seeking healing is to invite the muscle to tell us its story, to hear its side, possibly for the first time. We are here in the presence of the narrative ingredient so important in myth and dreams. As the story unfolds, and in subsequent reflection on the story, Tom recognizes the character represented by the headache and its symbol, the muscle, as his physiological stress responses, which he has learned to repress in the interests of his rationally oriented ego.

The third character is Christ. Here Tom responds to one of the archetypal symbols of divine intervention into human life. Christ represents the possibility of healing the symptom of the headache. But Christ is much more than that to Tom. He represents the partially known but obscured motivation for his life's vocation in ministry and in personal development. The motivation is so strong that it has led him into its service even though it has not been consciously experienced until now. Christ represents the greater power of authority and wisdom which Tom's ego acknowledges, to which he wishes to surrender, and to which he has resisted surrendering until now. We notice that the nature of the surrender of the ego to Christ is a mutual partnership, exhibited in the meditation in which the two depart laughing together, and in the therapy session in which the two embrace. Tom's ego is ready to enter into the mythic realm because it can enter as a full partner in the interactions taking place there. Tom is also able to go into the unknown realm because of the trustworthiness of Christ. Jung spoke of Christ as a symbol of the Self, of the capacity for the totality of the human potentiality to manifest. For Tom, that representation is clearly the case. He trusts Christ, and Christ is trustworthy as a guide to wholeness. This is a theme to which we will return. In my work with many individuals in Christian meditation and inner healing, I have been struck by the trustworthiness of the inner Christ and the healthy advice given by the inner Christ, when cultivated through these meditative practices.

Healing is symbolized by the joint drinking of the cup by both Tom and the knotted muscle. Both the identified rationality and the identified physical stress symptoms stand in need of wisdom and nourishment from a source more powerful than themselves. Does the Christ represent the return of the power of the gods to make that direct intervention from the realm beyond time and space, the same function that they served in the ancient myths and in Scripture? I believe so. It is interesting that Tom experienced an alteration in his sense of time and the recovery of long forgotten memories, indicating the possibility of an alteration in the perception of space. He has visited a realm within himself that differs in time and space from ordinary rational consciousness, a realm in which the divine and the demonic can speak and reveal themselves.

There is a fourth character, a yet hidden one, represented in the person of the therapist. The therapist represents an observing capability, a unifying capability, able to explore all the divergent parts and sense their mutual interaction. This capability is evoked in the subject through therapeutic and meditative experience. This observer represents the capacity of consciousness itself to expand and to contain paradox, the gods (like Christ) and the identified demons (like the headache and its knotted muscle), as well as one's own conscious ego-self. Jung spoke of this capability within the individual as the Self, distinguishing it from the limited consciousness of the ego. I suggest that "trust in God" means that we can also trust in the capacity of the Self to unify all the disparate and quarreling parts within us. The work of the soul is the work that Jung described as the creation of an ego-Self axis: a capacity of our consciousness to expand into the infinite potentialities of the Self and return to the daily concerns of the ego regarding life in time and space. It is our task both to identify the quarrelling inner powers and to bring them into communication with each other. Only thereby can intrapsychic healing occur. Hope is given for this process by our ultimate trust in the benevolent nature of the universe and the healing potential of the soul. God is the Self or Soul of the universe.

THE ART OF ENSOULING:
AN EXCURSION TO THE FOURTEENTH CENTURY

The soul as cavernous treasury, the soul as container of healing through dream, symbol, and metaphor, seems very distant from the self-understanding of contemporary Western humankind. We have been tricked by the empirical worldview into believing its principles: reality is only contained in that which the senses can perceive and the rational mind can construct. Yet, we know that while this represents one part of our reality, it cannot account for the longings of the heart for peace. It cannot account for the night struggles with meaning and purpose. It cannot account for the interior forces of light and darkness that are not perceived through the senses at all, but rather through inner imagination, through feeling states, and through physical symptoms of distress. We must construct a different worldview to make sense of Tom's experience, and of our own experiences in the inner realms of dreams, intuitions, and meditation. Where shall we begin?

While there are many models of the soul with which we might begin, I would like to take us on an excursion to fourteenth-century Europe. We will journey to that time in which the individual was given the sense of exalted dignity of which the author of *The Cloud of Unknowing* speaks, in which the human soul was understood to be capable of being in communication with all the forces of the universe. We will explore the world of Dante. His view of reality continues to influence us unconsciously and represents a high point in Western thought, integrating the medieval worldview with a highly developed psychological and mystical experience.

The *Divine Comedy* by Dante Alighieri is a monumental work of ensouling. Dante wrote the work while in exile from his native Florence. In the *Divine Comedy* Dante holds before us a graphic visual representation of the realms of the soul, as understood by his time. The three-part division of hell, purgatory, and paradise conforms to the mythic structure of his Christian worldview. But within this structure, Dante presents his own visionary experiences, freely assigning saints and scoundrels to the places of his liking, and freely interpreting the history of his day within the cosmic scheme. While the basic three-part division of hell, purgatory, and heaven was a part of the given cosmic scheme, Dante has done more than simply pin his time and place upon it. One has very much the sense that Dante is deeply entering into the questions of his own existence and

28

actually *formulating* the structure of reality for himself out of these deeply asked questions. Throughout the work, questions are asked relating to the nature of the soul, to the circumstances in which he finds various souls, and to the nature of divine revelation. His search begins when his worldview and relation to reality fall into ruin.

> Midway this way of life we're bound upon,
> I woke to find myself in a dark wood,
> Where the right road was wholly lost and gone.
>
> Ay me! how hard to speak of it — that rude
> and rough and stubborn forest! the mere breath
> of memory stirs the old fear in the blood;
>
> It is so bitter, it goes nigh to death;
> Yet there I gained such good, that, to convey
> The tale, I'll write what else I found therewith.
>
> How I got into it I cannot say,
> Because I was so heavy and full of sleep
> When first I stumbled from the narrow way; . . .
>
> And as a swimmer, panting, from the main
> Heaves safe to shore, then turns, to face the drive
> Of perilous seas, and looks, and looks again,
>
> So, while my soul yet fled, did I contrive
> To turn and gaze on that dread pass once more
> Whence no [one] yet came ever out alive.
> (Dante, *L'Inferno*, I:1-25, 1949, 71)

The *question* thrusts Dante into a new relationship with his soul, into an exploration of his worldview, and into the task of reconciling himself to his new reality. The way is fraught with fear, yet he determines to enter this wholly unknown realm. His way toward paradise is blocked and he must instead go through hell and purgatory. He cannot escape the realms of death and destruction.

Dante makes of his search a creative act of ensouling. Dante's guides into the realms of death are his beloved Beatrice and the poet of classical Rome, Virgil. In both cases, Dante allows his own psychic urgings to take precedence over any other convention of his day. Dante gives a place of honor to each of the major known authors of the classical world, in addition to Virgil, thus making a link between his Christian worldview and that of the ancients (Campbell

1968b, 107-8). That Beatrice is his guide into the heavenly realms of paradise represents a major shift in the Western psyche. The ideals of courtly love emerged in both European and Islamic culture during the twelfth to fourteenth centuries. This emergence of courtly, idealized love coincided with the honoring of the Virgin Mary and the building of great cathedrals to her honor (ibid., chap. 2). In Dante, this new feminine guide is not merely a spirit guide, but the same woman in death who has stirred his heart in life. Their love has become fully integrated into his Christian framework. Indeed, Dante presents a new image of that framework. It is by looking into Beatrice's face, into her radiance, that he gains the stamina to receive the direct radiance of God. Dante looks to Beatrice as his guide. She is his intermediary to divine radiance and mystical union. Dante's unique individuality and the unique qualities of his soul are evident in his relationship to Beatrice and to Virgil.

The realm of Dante's world especially related to the task of ensouling is purgatory. In purgatory, souls have an opportunity to purify themselves and to make themselves ready for the ecstatic bliss of paradise. In purgatory, individuals purify their interior attitudes through meditation exercises. These meditations are highly associated with transgressions of relationship. Those in purgatory stand in between their own interior perceptions and attitudes of enmity and their hurtful actions to others. Their meditation exercises cause them to realize their true nature as intermediate and responsible beings.

Dante's view of the soul involves several characteristics that we would do well to observe as we undertake to recapture the sense of life as the process of ensouling. Dante's discussion of the soul in purgatory presents a developmental model, which accounts for the association of human life with the natural world and with the spiritual world, thus creating the ability to be intermediate being (Dante, *Il Purgatorio*, XXV:49-78, 1955, 264-65). In the embryo's development, it passes through stages of identification with plant life and with animal life. When the brain has been completed, it is ready to receive the unique impress of God upon it, which enables it to return to God. Dante knows such a relationship to God in his visionary experiences in paradise. There he speaks of images of light, of radiance, and of the plenitude of saints and angels in splendor. In paradise, he holds true again to the science of his day, locating these realms in the heavens. Dante's concept of soul fulfills the requirements of soul that have been thus far set forth: soul represents an intermediate realm between nature and divinity, it is an imaginal realm, it moves from events in the world into a deepening of experience, and it seeks the common thread between interior motivation and exterior behaviors.

The most obvious problem for us, of course, is that Dante's soul rests on an outdated scientific viewpoint. However, I suspect that the main problem contemporary readers would have with Dante is not his science, which can be forgiven, but his mystical experience. It is tempting to think along these lines: Dante's world is based on a theory of the soul and of the universe that I no longer hold; therefore, his reported experience must be invalid or at least not available to me. Such thinking, however, confuses the experience of the psyche with the conceptual framework used to try to describe that experience. Jung, Hillman, and many others (cf. Bettelheim 1977; Singer 1973; Wilber 1980) are pointing out to us that the experiences of mythic thinking still go on within the human psyche, the experiences of mystical insight are still available. We have, however, pushed them underground, into the unconscious, from which they break through to us in dreams and psychopathologies. That such mythic and sometimes mystic experience can be available to us is demonstrated in the healing of the knotted muscle and the encounter with a very living presence of Christ that Tom experienced. Is it possible to formulate a contemporary framework for ensouling that gives us a superstructure analogous to Dante's hell, purgatory, and heaven, a framework with which to understand our life experiences as the process of the soul coming to consciousness?

ENSOULING: THE ART OF TRANSPERSONAL PSYCHOLOGY

As a contemporary discipline, psychology is a relative newcomer, emerging from the work of Sigmund Freud at the beginning of the twentieth century. As the art of ensouling, psychology is as old as humanity. It has been the art of storytellers, mothers and fathers, of shamans, artists, philosophers, and priests. Psychology is above all simply self-reflection, the task of reflecting upon myself. Psychotherapy involves another person in my self-reflection. Its most basic purpose is to serve the soul. "Let us recall here that psychotherapy, in accordance with the root meaning of the words 'psyche' and 'therapy' means to *serve soul*, not to treat it" (Hillman 1975, 74).

The context for the process of ensouling is vitally important. Does our view of the psyche contain the possibility for accommodating Tom's experience? Is it possible for us

31

to include the realm of divinity, as well as the influence of powerful and seemingly independent entities within our self-understanding, such as the demonic torture that Tom's knotted muscle represents? If our psychology does not make room for an understanding of experiences from the realms of myth, dreams, and mystic experience, then we have ceased to "serve the soul," and have instead "squeezed the soul" into our limited image.

Since the mid-1960s, the field of transpersonal psychology has been seeking to develop an understanding of the human psyche that can accommodate the experiences we have been describing. There are many contributors to this emerging psychology which gives us again a model of the soul. Carl Jung's seminal work laid the foundation for a return of soul into Western thinking. His work with mythology, with alchemy, with dreams and archetypes, and his postulation of the collective unconscious as the common psychological ground of us all have created a point of dialogue between psychology and religious concerns that continues to be very rich. Roberto Assagioli has elucidated a model of consciousness that speaks of the capacity for higher consciousness as well as the exploration of unconscious forces within us. His work has also contributed greatly to the use of imagination for the development of inner awareness. William James, early in this century, held forth the realm of religious experience as a proper realm for psychological examination. Recent work by key theoreticians, Ken Wilber, Stanislav Grof, Charles Tart, and practitioners such as Frances Vaughan and June Singer have contributed to this widening body of knowledge and information on the ways of the soul.

The term "transpersonal" has the connotation of going through the personal to that which is *beyond* the personal (Walsh and Vaughan 1980, 177). "Trans" also has the connotation of movement, change, fluidity. A transpersonal theory of ensouling acknowledges an inner integrity throughout the layers and levels of the known and unknown within the individual. We are coming back to Hillman's description of the primary tool for ensouling to be metaphor. *Whatever* is presented to my consciousness may become a guide to lead me into the depths of my life's meaning. It is the task of transpersonal psychology to elucidate a model of consciousness, which accurately portrays the conscious and unconscious realms within the individual, and to show how we may traverse these realms, thereby discerning the unique meaning and pattern of our lives.

A principle of transpersonal psychology is that the individual contains within him- or herself the capacity for self-healing. A therapeutic or healing context is one in which the hope that an individual can come into greater health is held before one who is in distress. Healing occurs as the individual begins to contact that source of inner wholeness within him- or herself (Walsh and Vaughan 1980, 183).

At first glance, such a stance seems to fly in the face of the historical Western viewpoint of sin, in which it is postulated that the individual is cut off from his or her original potential for health and can be restored to that health only through divine intervention. Transpersonal psychology would recognize that postulation as one view for describing the sense of separation and alienation that draws people into isolation and despair. It would inquire into the intrapsychic realities that cause us to postulate such a doctrine. And there, within ourselves, we do find a sense of division and of separation. Do we also, however, find the source of divine healing? In the mystical literature of the West as well as of the East, such a divine center of health and healing is reported. How can we account for such transcendent experience? One of the reasons that transpersonal psychology has become an identified field of study is to research the phenomena of reported transcendent experience and to assist us in attaining the health associated with such experience. Transpersonal psychology accepts Dante's visions as a form of human experience potentially available to us all. The specific contents of the visions, as well as the metaphysical framework into which we would place them, however, may be unique to individuals and cultures.

JUNG'S SELF AND THE SOUL

The term "transpersonal" was first used by Jung in early references to what he came to call the collective or impersonal unconscious. For Jung, there was the known, popularly called the "I" or the ego, and the unknown. The unknown, for Jung, consisted of both the unknown in the outer world, and knowable through the senses, and the unknown within the inner world. The "unconscious" is that which is unknown within the inner world (Jung 1968, 9-II, §2). For Jung, the ego, the "I," is simply the "centre of the field of consciousness . . . . The ego is the subject of all personal acts of consciousness. Theoretically, no limits can be set to the field of consciousness, since it is capable of indefinite extension" (ibid., §1-2). The movement of our souls is from that of which we are already conscious into an exploration of that which is as yet unknown or unconscious. We may explore that which is unknown about our own personal history, which forms the contents of the personal unconscious. And we may venture into the unknown that is common to all humanity in the collective or impersonal unconscious.

For Jung this impersonal and collective substrate of the psyche is the realm of the archetypes. We might liken this realm to the existence of DNA in the physical organism, a generalized plan out of which the individual takes its pattern of growth and development. That I am a human being and not a dog is a result of this impersonal, archetypal genetic code. However, that I am brown-haired and blue-eyed with a certain configuration of fat and muscle is dependent on my personal (though largely unconscious) genetic inheritance. Similarly, Jung proposes that the patterns of psychic structure for human beings are universal patterns (ibid., §12). In spite of the similarity of psychic substructure, human beings are characterized by a great capacity for uniqueness. The great themes are given in the substratum of the collective unconscious, common to all humanity, and so in that sense they are impersonal. Yet each of these themes or archetypes finds expression in a unique way in our individual lives.

"Individuation" is the term that Jung gave to the process of becoming conscious of our own uniqueness. To become truly individual, we must become conscious of what for Jung was the larger center of personhood, what he called, the "Self." The Self is finally unknown, reaching fully into the substratum of collective archetypes, yet it is knowable in part (Jung 1968, 9-II, §9). The first task of ensouling is to become aware that there is a greater Self within than we consciously know. Do we identify ourselves, our "I," merely with our habitual ways of being, or do we dare to address ourselves to the unknown within? The Self for Jung is the bridge between the personal "I" and the infinite potentiality represented by the collective substratum. This Self in Jung is very close to the lost soul for which we have been looking. When energy is freed from merely personal concerns, it becomes available for the exploration of this collective realm. "The primordial images are the most ancient and the most universal 'thought-forms' of humanity. They are as much feelings as thoughts; indeed, they lead their own independent life rather in the manner of part-souls" (Jung 1966, 7, §104). To begin to discover one's own archetypal patterns, from this deeper substratum of collective human patterns, is to begin to find one's lost soul.

A TRANSPERSONAL MODEL FOR ENSOULING

One of the most significant contributors to current theory in transpersonal psychology is Ken Wilber. Drawing upon cross-cultural views of human consciousness, he has devised a diagram of human development and human consciousness that accounts for the realms of the soul we have been exploring (see Figure 1). Represented in the diagram are both the process of ego-development so important to Western psychology and the process of ego-transcendence, which is the primary task of spiritual traditions, East and West.

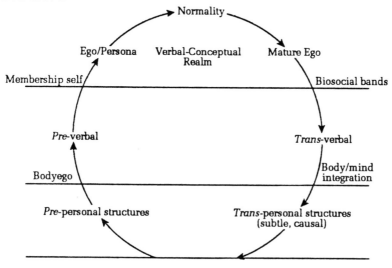

Highlights of the Life-Cycle: Pre- vs. Trans-

Figure 1
(Adapted by permission of the publisher from
Ken Wilber, *The Atman Project*
[Wheaton, Ill.: Theosophical Publishing House,
Quest Books, 1980], p. 50)

The movement in this diagram is from birth represented on the left in an upward arc of development aimed toward creating a stable ego structure. Wilber calls this movement "evolution." The individual is evolving from the unitive experience in the womb toward a sense of uniqueness and separation from other unique beings in the ego. After full egoic development, there comes a process that Wilber calls "involution," where the goal is a return to cosmic unity, which we will each experience in death.

The child develops a sense of separate identity first through identification with his or her body. At first the mental processes manifest as a sense of magical thinking, in which there is not a clear distinction between oneself and the outside world. This magic perception gives way by preschool age to a primitive form of mythic thinking. Through stories, myths, legends, and fairy tales, children are learning the beliefs of the society into which they have been born. For this reason Wilber also calls this stage of development "membership cognition." Children learn to think and perceive reality through the perceptions of those around them. With the beginning of rational development, children begin to think on their own, to be able to reflect upon the community in which they have membership. It is with the development of this capability for experiencing oneself isolated not only from the created world, but also from one's own group, that the universal sense of alienation and isolation arises. Wilber identifies this sense of isolation with the development of ego awareness, or awareness of oneself as a separate being.

Once the egoic function is in place, which insures the ability to survive as an adult in a quite complex environment, and once that survival has been proven, the primary work of the ego is completed. What often happens in our culture at that point is identified as an existential crisis. One's life goals seem fulfilled, yet one is painfully empty. The energy of evolution has been expended. Our attention turns toward the ultimate questions of our existence. Needleman's question calls us. We become aware that our life is moving toward death and a return to union with all the levels of reality from which we separated in order to establish our sense of uniqueness as an ego. The existential crisis is the call to consciously enter into the process of ensouling.

> Midway this way of life we're bound upon,
>   I woke to find myself in a dark wood,
>   Where the right road was wholly lost and gone.
>   (Dante, *L'Inferno*, I:1, 1949, 71)

Wilber's model is useful in describing the similarity between the mythic thinking of childhood and the imaginal world of ensouling into which we enter as adults. "Mythic thinking, *in its mature forms*, is not at all pathological or distortive, but rather joins with the higher phantasy (of vision-image) to disclose depths of reality and high modes of archetypal being quite beyond ordinary logic" (Wilber 1980, 24). As children develop, they unconsciously absorb their cultural myths and seek to live by them. The mature ego has now the capacity to perceive the archetypal structures underlying the myths and fairy tales of childhood and begins to enter into a direct and conscious relationship with these archetypal figures. At the height of maturity in adulthood, the *question*, existentially presented in despair, lack of meaning, or in the terror of dreams, calls us back into relationship with the imaginal realm beyond logic. The realm of soul is this realm in which the work of our lives is an inner work, rediscovering the capacity for myth and moving through the mythic world into relationship with archetypal energies. The unconscious motivations for our lives become conscious. In the case of our client, the hidden Christ becomes present, and the demon discloses itself. I suggest that the realm between the lines on Wilber's chart is the realm in which we begin to awaken the soul. I would summarize the discoveries of this chapter in Figure 2. The figure illustrates the interaction between the types of inner experience, such as reason, imagination, and contemplative radiance, and when those types of consciousness are most likely to be present in the developmental stages of individual human life.

We experience our lives as a movement from the Spirit, from radiance in the womb and unitive experiences of infancy, into the early childhood period of ensouling, in which we receive our tools for ego-development. Wilber identifies the ego mentality with the hero, the individual in conflict and in battle (Wilber 1981b, 182-87). Fairy tales provide the child a mythical structure for ego development. We find in them maps for development into ego maturity. "It is important to provide the modern child with images of heroes who have to go out into the world all by themselves and who, although originally ignorant of the ultimate things, find secure places in the world by following their right way with deep inner confidence" (Bettelheim 1977, 11). The fairy tales and mythic stories of early childhood need to provide this framework.

When we return to this nonlogical mind in mature adulthood, we will often encounter unresolved issues from that early childhood development. These are best communicated to us through myth-like stories. In this magic kingdom there can be an interaction between the mythic realm of childhood and the archetypal figures of mature or high phantasy. To illustrate the healing possibilities of such interaction, let us return to Tom's experience. The knotted

37

muscle, representative of the repressed physical sensations, a condition most likely set into motion in early childhood, speaks to us in a form that is much like the child's mythic world. It also has magical powers and can present us with memories. It functions as an entity with its own personality. Healing takes place when we allow it to tell us its story. The story involves an interaction among three powerful figures, that of the logical ego, Christ, and the demonic muscle. Each represents a powerful archetypal messenger from the client's depths. Healing is established by their entering into community with each other.

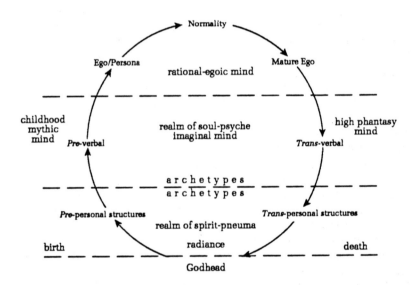

Figure 2
(Adapted from Wilber, 1980)

If we successfully navigate the troubled waters of beginning inner healing processes, we come to a new way of being, in which there is genuine body/mind integration. Tom's inner work reveals conflicts between body and rational mind that need resolution. Healing comes as he learns to listen to his physical being and learns to respond directly. Such body/mind integration work will be prominent for many of us in our inner healing process.

In the bottom right area of Wilber's map of consciousness, the transpersonal structures see us approaching death. Wilber has characterized the two major types of transpersonal structures to be experiences of the "subtle" realm and of the "causal" realm. While these structures manifest as we approach death, they are also accessible to us in our interior meditative prayer experience. These terms are taken from Buddhism, but they have strong correlates in Christian mystical literature. Subtle realm experience is the realm of prayer healing in which Christ or Mary or another powerful divine intermediary figure is present. In subtle realm experience, the divine takes form. It is an arena in which we will do much exploring, particularly in the imaginational use of the healing stories of Jesus and in the use of the Eastern Orthodox Jesus Prayer.

In causal realm experience we "dwell" with God as such. It is a realm of formless radiance. Dante's experience in paradise illustrates the passage through the subtle realm to the causal realm. In the higher rungs of paradise, Dante sees the saints in splendor, as well as the apostles. These are the divine in form. Beatrice is his mediator to the direct approach to God. The divine splendor is envisioned as light approached in greater and greater intensity. The light is too bright for Dante. Beatrice looks directly at God's radiance, and Dante looks into her face until he gradually grows accustomed to the radiance. Then, he looks into the divine radiance directly. And there he leaves off his narrative to "penetrate into the Primal Love" (Dante, *Il Paradiso*, XXXII:142, 1962, 338). Wilber describes the causal realm as the Christian world of *pneuma*, pure spirit. It is a world where the mystics have tread before us and into which we may find ourselves venturing as well. It is the divine beyond form. It is the realm of radiant light or of divine dark. It is a realm where the more advanced practice of the Jesus Prayer tends to lead us. The practice of Centering Prayer, as described in *The Cloud of Unknowing*, is designed to assist us to dwell in this realm of "no-thing-ness" and deeply appropriate divine love. These realms also well describe what many people experience as they move toward death. One of the most moving experiences of my teaching was reading some of the mystical descriptions of divine love experienced in contemplation to a group of older persons. A woman of advanced years spoke up with delight in her voice and reported to the group that the description put into words what she had experienced "when she had died." Her experience of clinical death was described in a twelfth-century meditator's experience, when he enjoyed "the sweetness of divine contemplation, not drop by drop, not now and then, but in an unceasing flow of delight which no one shall take away, an unchanging peace, the peace of God" (Guigo II 1978, 99).

The Christian mystical tradition has spoken of the process of ensouling as initially quite traumatic, during which there are alternations between periods of illumination and of purification. In fact, this initial stage is often called "purgation" (Underhill 1961). I suggest that the natural response of the soul to an infusion of energy or insight from the causal realms or simply from the relaxation of egoic tensions is to dredge up repressed material from the childhood mythic mind. These monsters of the deep contain within themselves the clues to unlock the pathologies of our bodies as well as of our emotions.

We begin the process of ensouling by allowing the questions of our existence to disidentify us from our rational-egoic image of ourselves (Assagioli 1977, 22-24). We are thereby freed to begin giving attention to other voices within ourselves: the voices of dreams, the voices of physical distresses, the voices of our despairs and ecstasies and of the ultimate meaning of our lives. Through such attention to the unknown within ourselves we begin to shift our center of consciousness from the known to a new middle ground, a new point of intermediacy among all the forces within ourselves. Jung spoke of a "mid-point of the personality" that could assimilate information from the unconscious. With the development of this mid-point, one's center of awareness shifts from the ego to the new mid-point. "This would be the point of new equilibrium, a new centering of the total personality, a virtual centre which, on account of its focal position between conscious and unconscious, ensures for the personality a new and more solid foundation" (Jung 1966, 7, §365).

This new mid-point of personality is the soul-in-formation, illustrated in Figure 3. Ensouling consists of extending our capacity for attention to all parts of our total being, including the inner realms of repression and unknown radiance. The logic-egoic structure then becomes the bridge between the inner soul and the external world. The soul needs that center as its reference point in time and space. But the center of the person is no longer ruled by time and space, or by the contingencies of the world of sense perception. In the language of Jung, our center becomes no longer simply our conscious knowledge of ourselves; our center becomes the Self, bridging our consciousness into the personal and collective unconscious.

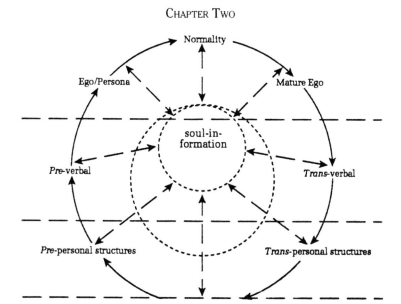

Figure 3
(Adapted from Wilber, 1980)

In this chapter, I have sought to present a structure of human experience that allows for the recovery of the soul. I have sought to present the possibility for the creation of ourselves as intermediate beings, again poised between the world of sense perception and the radiance of the eternal dimension. Let us now turn to the practices of Christian meditation and the processes of inner healing that enable us to move forward with hope through the "vale of soulmaking" called the world.

CHAPTER THREE

Christian Meditation and Spiritual Development

As we begin our practice of Christian meditation, it is help-ful to have an understanding of general principles of meditation. In this chapter, the processes of meditation as expressed in a variety of religious and secular modes will be discussed. Within this larger scheme of meditation prac-tices, we will then be able to place the practice of Christian meditation. This context will also enable us to speak of the relationship between Christian meditation and prayer. We will discuss movement along the ego-Self axis as described by Jung, exploring the types of inner experience we can expect to encounter in our meditation practice. I will am-plify this discussion of interior reality with the exploration of the ego-world axis, showing the interrelationship between our inner and exterior life. Finally, a more extensive discus-sion of the stages of spiritual growth to be expected as we undertake an interior personal practice such as Christian meditation will conclude the chapter.

CONCENTRATION, MINDFULNESS, AND MIXED MEDITATION PRACTICES

As we survey the types of practices that have been called meditation throughout the world's religions and more re-cently under the guise of relaxation and stress management, clearly anything can be the object of meditation. Similar psychological and physiological processes occur whenever we take a certain mental stance toward any object. Medita-tion practices have literally run from the most diffuse and universal, such as meditation on the 'is-ness' of God, to the most concrete, such as meditation on a corpse.

In general, meditation practices may be described either as meditation on an object or meditation on the inner process of the meditator. Meditation on an object is described as concentration meditation. Meditation on the inner process of the meditator is described as mindfulness meditation. A third category is described as mixed, simultaneously utilizing principles of both concentration and mindfulness practices. An excellent resource for a full discussion of these distinctions is Daniel Goleman's *The Meditative Mind.*

Mindfulness meditation, or meditation on the inner process of the meditator, is described in the styles of Zen meditation associated with simply being present to the passing moment. Mindfulness meditation in another Buddhist variation known as Vipassana, or insight meditation, is well described in Joseph Goldstein's *The Experience of Insight.* Briefly, mindfulness meditation may be described as taking the approach to our inner experience of a camera's wide-angle lens. The purpose of such practice is to learn the habits of thought and emotional responses by which we are conditioned. The premise is that we create much of our own suffering through ignorance of our inner processes. For example, we react with outrage to some of the simplest indiscretions of others. That outrage makes us miserable and, if expressed, may also create misery for those around us. What has triggered us? The principles of mindfulness meditation are that as we become conscious of such patterns, we can change them and no longer be victimized by our own unconscious inner dynamics.

Concentration meditation may be likened to the telephoto lens of the camera. With concentration practice, we may explore unique "states" of mind. For example, if we concentrate on a corpse we would expect our inner experience to be very different from our experience if we concentrate on a candle flame. Both are practices within Hindu tradition. Tibetan Buddhist practice has created a virtually limitless array of specific concentration practices that are prescriptive for various emotional issues. There are meditations on different colors, shapes, sounds, and mythic figures that can be suggested depending on the areas of difficulty of the meditator.

In its pure form concentration meditation takes us "out" of the present moment and into eternity. To use the categories we have been discussing in the realms of the soul, concentration meditation enables us to move into subtle and causal realm experience. Even if the object is a natural object, with pure concentration, we eventually are drawn toward the ground of eternity from which the object sprang. A criticism of pure concentration meditation practice is that we can learn to go to specific places in our soul, but we can neglect to integrate that experience with other messages from within. In fact, we can learn to ignore certain parts of ourselves. An example from everyday life common to many people will illustrate this danger. Anne related her experience of working for sixteen years in a technologically sophisticated environment, with sound near the maximum allowed by law and limited spectrum lighting. She realizes now that she trained herself to shut out the negatives of the environment and the physical stress she was experiencing to concentrate on the product on which she was working. She now feels that those years of ignoring her physical stress reactions to the environment have created a major health problem for her. It is also useful to note that we must learn some degree of concentration to accomplish anything. It is a very important aspect of our internal life. For this reason, the teaching of mindfulness meditation practice begins with learning concentration meditation, for example, counting breaths.

It is intriguing to note that Christian meditation practices are primarily concentration practices. They work especially at the task of opening our ego-mind to be receptive to Christ as inner healer, or to take us into the adoration of God as "primal love." They primarily take us into a new relationship with eternity, from which we then have a new relationship with everyday life. The key mystic writers in Christian tradition always speak of the need to ground the interior meditative experience in external life. They are building in the necessary counterbalance to concentration meditation practice. St. Teresa of Avila puts this need most clearly when she writes that wherever we go within the interior castle of the soul, whatever rooms we explore, we should never leave the house of self-knowledge. I take this to mean that we should also be cultivating a mind of mindfulness. We should be looking for the interrelationships within our interior experience. We should also always be looking to expand our consciousness of ourselves. For Teresa the reason was simple: the better we know ourselves, the better able we will be to express compassion.

In *The Soul's Journey into God* (Cousins 1978), St. Bonaventure begins his spiritual exercises with an elaborate exploration of the natural faculties of the individual. Before one turns to contemplate Christ, one has already contemplated the natural universe, one's own capacities as a creature of senses, reason, imagination, and feeling.

44

Bonaventure has systematically built in the process of mindfulness, the process of self-observation, before turning the contemplative loose to dwell in the ecstasy of God. From a somewhat different perspective but with similar results, Dante's purgatory is essential before entering paradise. In purgatory, one wrestles with one's moral life, with one's deepest motivations. One explores the "seven deadly sins," the attitudes of envy, pride, lust, greed, sloth, avarice, and hatred. That kind of exploration cannot be done without careful examination of our interior habits of thought and feeling.

There is a danger in Christian meditation practices. This danger has been especially associated with the Jesus Prayer. It can take us into such an identification with the eternal aspect of life that we lose sight of the practical and everyday. We must understand that the context of monastic life in which these practices were cultivated built in manual labor as a part of the daily routine. Individuals were also watched over by a spiritual guide, lest they lose sight of the goal of full integration of the personality, lest they forget that holiness is wholeness.

A safeguard for us as we undertake these practices is to use them in a mixed mode. That is the way I will be guiding us. While we will essentially be working with concentration forms of meditation, I will be asking us always to be mindful of the feelings, the memories, the physical sensations, and the moral dimensions of our interior motivations. I will also guide us in the grounding practice of observing our natural capacities, as described by Bonaventure.

A final word of caution is that meditation practices of any kind, including Christian meditation, can sometimes present images or memories to us that are painful. Sometimes we will need to go out of the privacy of our prayer closet and seek guidance from others. Sometimes it is enough to work these difficult issues through with journaling or painting or another form of expression. Sometimes we need to tell them. Sometimes we are in the grip of an unconscious story until we have heard ourselves tell the full story to another. In Chapter Eight we will discuss forms of journaling, spiritual counseling, and models for group spiritual direction as ways to assist in our processing of inner material.

MEDITATION AND PRAYER

A profound way to keep our balance in our inner journeys is continually to hold before ourselves the concerns of others. It is my thesis, as you will have noted, that we are essentially relational creatures. In seeking inner healing for a problem that plagues us, we will discover a relationship issue in the depths of that internal problem. Our life of meditation is not divorced from our life of prayer, but we might think of the two as the Mary and Martha of our concerns. Martha brings the concerns of others before God in prayer; Mary learns to contemplate the essence of God in silent receptivity.

Often as people begin a Christian meditation practice they have raised questions regarding the integration of the receptive practices of meditation within their prayer life. A very useful term has been given to this process of prayer and meditation in a book entitled, *Don't You Belong to Me?* It is authored anonymously by "A Monk of New Clairvaux" (1979), a Trappist community in Napa Valley, California. The author speaks of "active prayer and dispositional prayer." Active prayer is the term used to describe our ordinary understanding of prayer: prayers of intercession, petition, and confession. Here are the prayers of Martha, the concerns for self and others being offered to God. In active prayer, we form words, we offer concerns. There is activity on our part. God is the listener. Dispositional prayer is the term the author gives to forms of Christian meditation. In dispositional prayer, meditation is a tool to quiet our minds and hearts and "dispose" us to hear God. The activity is with God, and we seek simply to be receptive and to listen.

In my experience, these two forms of prayer alternate in a meaningful meditative prayer experience. If we have been used to offering active prayers, it may be necessary to begin our meditative prayer time by speaking our prayers to God. Only after we have stated our concerns can we begin to still our minds. Alternately, we may begin our meditation with a dispositional form, yet as we meditate concerns will come to mind. I suggest that we should definitely enter into a more active prayer form then, stating our prayers and concerns. After we have stated these concerns, we then return to the receptive mode. We are multidimensional beings. We are both active and receptive. We will find both dimensions surfacing in our meditative prayer life and we will wisely learn more facility with both.

Christian meditation, properly practiced, can be called dispositional prayer. Prayer is the cultivation of our relationship with God, the time set aside to enter consciously that relationship. Christian meditation is one mode of many that can be used to remember the divine source. It is the form of prayer in which we attend to God in receptive silence.

We recall that our task is to allow God to transform our whole being into hope, to transform body, mind, and heart into Godself. That transformative possibility is limited if we are always filling the channel to God with our concerns. That transformative possibility increases if we learn to listen to and to receive from God. For this reason, St. Teresa of Avila described the most profound transformative experiences for the individual as occurring in deep contemplative silence. Our practice of Christian meditation will enable us to enter this arena of transformative silence. It is the arena in which our wills become aligned with the divine will, in which our hearts are infused with divine hope, in which contemplative love heals us of the roots of sin.

JOURNEYING THE EGO-SELF AXIS, JOURNEYING THE EGO-WORLD AXIS

As we begin any practice of meditation, we find several dynamics at work. Let us return to the diagrams of the last chapter to begin to understand these potentials for inner work.

A clarification I would add to Wilber's model is that the "world" and all our external relationships lie at the top of the chart. We need the ego to relate to that world. The human faculty for relating to the exterior world is the senses. See Figure 4 for this corrective addition. So, through our own consciousness of the world, we bring its concerns into our inner life, and through our relationship to the depth dimensions within, we become the vehicle for the archetypes to speak through us to our present age. I have often thought of humankind as the heart of God in our world. If we take ourselves as intermediate beings seriously, humankind is that force that stands in relationship to "all that is" in a unique way, at least upon the earth. Our task is to be aware of what is happening here and through our prayers and the "inarticulate groans" of our hearts to let God know what is happening here. We play a vital unifying role within our own consciousness, as we seek to relate through the faculties to all the levels of being. Through such a perspective, the ego is redeemed from being limited to the rational

47

function and becomes instead a true window of the soul, a window to the inner depths and a window to the breadth of all our relationships.

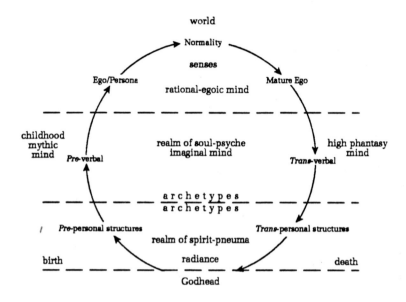

Figure 4
(Adapted from Wilber, 1980)

The ego-Self axis speaks to the inner dimension of this process. As we journey inwardly, as we make our journey toward God through the inner worlds, we encounter the world of rational thought as well as the world of imagination, of story, of psychological complex, of dreams, and of interiorized stresses. We may also journey to the pure perception of God through the formless contemplation of divine compassion or radiant light that characterizes experience in the causal realm. To learn to make that journey inward to these depths and back outward to our ego-in-relationship to the world is the function of the ego-Self axis. The spirituality our world needs now is not one that draws us out of the world, but one that empowers us to be within the world as people of hope. Our inner meditation practices will enable us to make these journeys back and forth between ego and Self. The capacity to make such journeys we have been calling the process of ensouling, a process of learning our depths and our interior symbolic language.

48

If our prayer life is truly to flourish, however, we must speak not only of an ego-Self axis but also of an ego-world axis. Can we also project our minds and hearts into the struggles for common life in our world? Can we relate to the ecological suffering of the world? Can we stand in the shoes of the homeless? The disciples of Jesus must cultivate this knowing heart in the world as well as in the interior regions of the Self.

To complete the map of the soul that we are developing, we must explore the complexity of the notion of the world. I am indebted to Baker Brownell (1950) for his understanding of the following levels of community. Brownell states that we must relate to each of these levels of community if we are to function in a healthy way in our world. These levels of relationship must each receive some of our attention.

The *phyletic* community is that stream of family through which we have been born. Our genus is *homo sapiens*, our *phylum* is the particular biological and cultural family into which we have been born. We stand in relationship to its inheritance to us and to the unborn future generations who claim us. Nowhere is the issue of hope stronger than in relationship to this community. Do we hear the claims of our ancestors still being worked out in us? Do we hear the claims of unborn future generations asking us to be responsible for our moment of human life, to honor the earth, and to leave her refreshed rather than depleted? Within the concerns of the phyletic community are our relationships to our parents and our children. These are mirrored in the inner world in the unfinished business we have from our childhood, issues that will often surface in meditation, issues that cry for healing, forgiveness, and reconciliation.

Another level of community is the natural community. How well do we relate to the environment, to all living creatures, to the air, the wind, the forests, and soil of life? We must ask these questions today. In our inner world these concerns are mirrored in our relationship to our bodies and the appreciation and honoring of our own natural capacities. Matthew Fox (1983), in his extensive work on creation spirituality, has led Christians to rethink their relationship to the natural beings that we are. We will find that the practice of "contemplative love" as voiced in *The Cloud of Unknowing* leads to a profound reconciliation with our own inner urges and physical life. We begin to honor nature by honoring our bodies and appreciating the senses.

A third type of community to which we need to relate for wholeness is the mystic community. In the external world this is the church or other communities of spiritually earnest folk. It is also that body of individuals, living and dead, to whom we look for inspiration. It is the "communion of saints" who inspire us. In the external world, these can be our mentors, teachers, and heroes. In our interior world, they can be our inner circle of spirit guides or the cultivated presence of Christ. Dante's circle of saints and apostles in paradise served this function, as well as his guides through the various realms. Our dream figures can serve this function as well. Do we allow ourselves to be inspired and guided by sources beyond ourselves in the external and the inner world?

Finally, there are the communities of the neighborhood and expanding circles of political and geographic communities that lead us through the city, to the state, the nation, the hemisphere, and the world social-political community. To each of these we owe a part of our attention, in each of these we are citizens. Each of these will call to us for prayer and action. Each of these is an arena for enacting the inspiration we receive from listening to God, and each of these groans for completion in hope.

Figure 5 illustrates the dynamics of both the ego-Self axis and the ego-world axis. It attempts to illustrate the full range of interior and exterior relationships that we bring into our prayer. The lower half of the figure recapitulates Wilber's model of consciousness, with the left side representing the range of issues we encounter in our process of developing into ego-consciousness. The lower right represents the types of issues and themes that can arise for us in mature spiritual growth. As we do our interior meditation work, we will find these arenas interacting with each other as a part of our inner healing.

The upper half of the figure correlates Brownell's categories of community with Wilber's model of interior development. For example, the relationship with the environment and ecological concern relates to our interior relationship with our bodies. The external relationship to the phyletic community relates to our own interior relationship to our early childhood experience in our families. The degree of political empowerment we express externally relates to our own interior myths of community and social life.

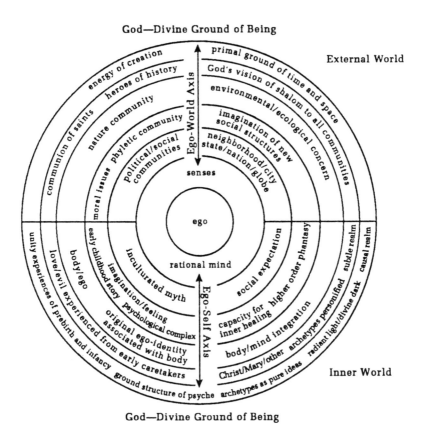

Figure 5
(Adapted from Wilber, 1980)

The key discovery of these correlations is that our inner and exterior worlds are inextricably interrelated. As we do our interior healing, we are healing our exterior relationships. As we address the suffering of the external world, we must also attend to our interior suffering. As we approach the deepest structures of either our inner world or the exterior world we find God at work envisioning a hopeful future.

51

We have thus further broadened our definition of ensouling to include attending to the ego-world axis as well as the ego-Self axis. All these penetrating interrelationships make up the world of soul-making in which we find ourselves. The haunting questions of life can come from any of these arenas. And the divine *shalom* discovered in our hearts links with the divine *shalom* of creative energy sustaining the world's life from moment to moment.

The soul-in-formation has now shifted from a merely interior process to one also encompassing the exterior world. We thereby begin to recover the exalted dignity of the human being, concerned with relating to all of creation.

MEDITATING AND PRAYING OVER ALL OUR RELATIONSHIPS

We bring to our prayer and meditation all our relationships. Nothing is excluded. We allow ourselves to address all our relationships because suffering is rooted in the conflict among these relationships. The Judeo-Christian understanding of God is that God has given a modicum of freedom to every created entity. That theological postulation has now found grounding in the science of quantum physics. There is a certain unpredictability of movement among the smallest particles of matter that can be detected. There is a certain freedom inherent in any created entity (Capra 1975). We constantly create suffering by exercising our authority at the expense of others. Whether we explore the interior suffering we have internalized from our early childhood experience, the momentary crisis of hostility that breaks out in our family quarrels, the suffering inflicted by nation upon nation or class upon class, or the injury humankind is perpetrating upon the earth's ecosystems, we encounter abuse of relationship. We need forgiveness for trespassing upon others. *Shalom, hesychasm,* our interior peace, is not possible without addressing peace in the world of relationships. The divine hope calls us because it promises such a universal peace. The promise of that peace is the ultimate question under which we struggle. That is the promised peace of Christ. Such peacemaking at every level is the practice of the redemption of the world.

This process is experienced most graphically in the Native American sweat lodge ceremony. The sweat lodge is a ceremonial arena for purification and prayer. Into the sweat lodge one brings one's struggles and pains. One looks for renewed hope and for guidance. The sweat lodge is prepared in such a way that each petitioner must enter crawling on one's knees. This act of humility and offering oneself to the Great Spirit is accompanied by saying the words: "All my relations." Into the sweat lodge, into the arena of prayer, one brings all one's relationships for healing. That includes the earth, family, society, and all one's interior pain. Our prayer and meditation are most meaningful when we bring all our relationships into the divine healing possibility.

Christian prayer has always countered the tendency of meditation to "bliss" us out of contact with the suffering of relationships by calling attention to the centrality of Christ's crucifixion. Christ died, Christ suffered. Our suffering and God's are inextricably interrelated. Jesus continuously calls our attention to the "least" among us. We cannot discern God's movements of hope and our place within them with blinders on our eyes.

In summary, Christian meditation and prayer call us not only to a mindfulness of our interior process, of the inter-relationships among our thoughts, feelings, physical sensations, and imaginative dreamings; we are also called to mindfulness of the interrelationships of the many levels of community in the exterior world in which we live. We bring all those concerns to prayer and meditation. We actively speak our concerns, our hurts, and our sufferings to God. And we learn to listen to God's hope, God's creative inspiration calling to us, claiming us for the renewal of the world.

STAGES OF SPIRITUAL DEVELOPMENT

Our discussion of ensouling and of the arenas to which we expand our attention possesses an inherent dynamic of development. Jung spoke of incorporating more and more of the unknown both within ourselves and our world into our consciousness. We have spoken of expanding our notion of who we are from our ego self-concept to that of "intermediate being," and to cultivating soul as the capacity to stand in relationship to all that is. Wilber's model itself is a theory of psychological and spiritual stages of development. The *Divine Comedy* describes Dante's understanding of the stages of spiritual development and assumes the descent into the darkness of hades and the moral purification of purgatory before entry into the ecstatic heights of paradise.

There are numerous models that we might explore, a project too extensive for the present. What I wish to do here is to give a glimpse of some of the possible guideposts that have been given historically to those who enter the arena of Christian meditation and inner healing. For this purpose we will speak briefly of the stages of development as described by Evelyn Underhill in Part II, "The Mystic Way," in her book, *Mysticism* (1961). Although written in 1911, *Mysticism* is surprisingly fresh in its presentation of the classical Western model of spiritual development.

Underhill elaborates on the model of spiritual development that has largely held the imagination of Christian mystics throughout history. The rudiments of the model have been attributed to the Greek philosopher Plotinus, who lived in the third century C.E. The threefold stages of Plotinus are purification, illumination, and unification of the individual with God. Underhill expands this model into the following stages: the awakening of the self, the purification of the self, the illumination of the self, the dark night of the soul, and the unitive life. This model has come under substantive criticism by Matthew Fox as resting too strongly on the sin-redemption tradition in Christianity. I have found Underhill's model, however, to contain a ring of psychological correctness and universal application. I will point out possible correctives from Matthew Fox's criticism as we go along.

This process of spiritual development assumes a mature adult, with a developed ego, with skills in interrelation to the world at large, yet who has come to realize that "there is more to life" than currently being lived. Underhill characterizes the experience of this "more" as the awakening of the self, what we might call, in the terms I have been developing, awakening to the soul. It is the realization that there is a profound truth to the faith promises of dwelling with God. Often such awakening is accompanied by a conversion, a new experience of divine presence. The awakening may be gradual, over a period of years, or sudden. To the positive sounding "conversion," I would add the fierce dimension of awakening that may come to us in the terror of dreams, the despair of closed doors, or the boredom of fulfilled tasks. The call of the soul may come from the unfulfilled possibilities that arouse us from complacency. The awakening of the self often manifests as the midlife crisis, which may come at any time from the late twenties to the fifties, the time when our ego structure weakens and we awake to the vastness of potential within and without us and grieve over the narrowness of our current life.

This awakening is a turning toward a new discovery of depth and divine inspiration. It may also be a time of initiating a regular meditative prayer practice. It is ordinarily followed by a period of major interior dislocation that Underhill calls the purification or purgation of the self. As we turn our attention toward that which has been unconscious and hidden within us, we will often find fierce forces at work. Jung called these forces, psychological complexes. They are emotional patterns that have begun very early in life and that have taken on a power of their own, so that they keep reinforcing themselves and in fact building power within our psychic structure. We will each have such complexes constellated around fear, perfection, failure, and our body image, to name only a few. As we begin the journey of ensouling, these, like Tom's painful headache, will cry out to us for attention. We will enter rather dramatically into Wilber's realm of imagination, wrestling with the demons of childhood. Often these complex patterns will become personified in dream figures or figures that will appear in our imaginative meditations; beneath the complexes, at a still deeper level the archetypes may call directly.

As one can imagine, this new depth of psychic life is usually difficult for our ego to handle. While we may have consciously longed for some change, we suddenly begin to get much more than we expected. Underhill underscores that this purification can be in the external world as well as in the inner world. Our purification may dawn as the loss of work, or a dramatic shift in relationships, or in deep questions of moral integrity. Whatever has been hidden comes to light for purification.

The stage of illumination offers a respite, if only in glimpses, from the chaos of purification. Illumination describes the inner experience of meditations of light, of direct perception of God, a period some authors describe as "infused prayer" and some describe as contemplation. The interior life of the individual finds a plateau of serenity and quiet. This is the stage where St. Teresa of Avila speaks of the greatest transformation of the individual occurring. In the silent depths, God directly begins to influence our heart, mind, body, and spirit. We begin to be turned fully toward God, in both our inner and exterior relationships. In Wilber's model, the work of body-mind integration is a bridge between the stages of purification and illumination. A part of our purification process is reclaiming our bodies, taking our conscious awareness back into our bodies. The process of purification may be accompanied by somewhat difficult physical distresses, as old pains are reopened and brought to healing light. As body and mind are cleared of the accumulated pain of living our lives in the grip of our unconscious complexes and patterns, a new clarity and simplicity of mind begin to emerge. A quieter body and a quieter mind emerge, which can rest in God. The celebrative center is discovered, and we learn to dwell in it.

For Underhill, there can be a lengthy period of oscillation between purification and illumination. In fact, I suggest that oscillation is the place we will mostly live our mature spiritual lives. For as soon as a new equilibrium is reached, the creative hope of God reaches into our beings with a new question, and we are plunged into a round of purification, seeking new light on the suffering of ourselves or others.

For some few, as attested in the Western mystical literature, there may be a particularly deep purification, described as the dark night of the soul. Here, we are in the realm of total surrender to God and total transformation of the personality, the motivations, the actions, and the will of the individual into God. That process has been especially described in the very late stages of life. It is the process that has been usually associated with sainthood. The end is life in union with God, the unitive life, as Underhill describes it, wherein day by day, moment by moment, the divine expresses itself through the individual.

The dark night of the soul is a purification that takes the individual to the essence of life and to confrontation with death. Every aspect of life is questioned. Every problematic is explored. St. John of the Cross described three stages to the dark night (Kavanaugh and Rodriguez 1973, 75). The first is the dark night of the senses, wherein sensual pleasure ceases. In its most dramatic cases there is actually a cessation of active association of the individual with the pleasures of senses such as taste and touch and sight. In a less dramatic version of this experience, we may say the things of the senses become less important. Before the awesome experience of divine presence the mundane loses its attraction.

The middle stage is called the dark night of the soul by St. John of the Cross. By soul, John means the mental capacities of the individual: the reasoning, imagining, feeling capacities. In the dark night of the soul, a radical transformation of our interior motivations and structures of thought and feeling occurs.

The final stage, which John equates with the period of the night just before dawn, he calls the dark night that is God. By this he means that one's total consciousness has entered into God. Thus there is darkness that will become dawn, from which fresh motivation and creativity will spring.

And what is the unitive life? St. Teresa ends the *Interior Castle* by asking the purpose of the inner transformation. Her answer is "good works, good works." For Teresa, the purpose of this whole journey of interior transformation is manifest in our life of service in the world. The fruit of the awakening of the self is increased compassion. There is a difference, however, for Teresa in the quality of her good works before and after this interior awakening. The way has been cleared for God to align directly with the individual, for love to flow through a unified will. The struggle between God's will and the individual's will has ceased. Thus, there is a serenity of the individual. And, Teresa says, she rarely forgets God. There is an abiding presence, undergirding and guiding her.

The corrective that Matthew Fox rightly offers to this description is that it tends to lead to a negation of the sensual world. He suggests that we must keep ourselves balanced by coming back repeatedly to the affirmation of the goodness of creation, or what he calls the *via positiva*, to balance the purgative work. Our creativity emerges from the balance of the positive with the suffering dimension of our lives. This creativity, for Fox, must also be given expression in the world as a part of the transformation of the world. These principles have been amply with us already, and we will continue to hold them in balance with the more classical model of transformation into God.

As we begin our meditation work together, I will hold Fox's positive corrective before us. We need not only to focus on our interior struggles but keep ourselves alive to the sensory world. I will begin our practice with a wonderful exercise of exploring a positive relationship to nature. We will then work with scriptural meditation in ways that utilize both our reason and our imagination. Next we will turn to the Jesus Prayer, which takes us into the subtle and causal realms. Finally, we will explore Centering Prayer as described in *The Cloud of Unknowing*, a bridge into both the causal realm and into the world. The simplicity of Centering Prayer really forms the basic attitude for all our prayer, cultivating the attitude of contemplative love, an attitude and feeling of compassion both to ourselves and to all the world.

Let us begin to wrap ourselves in this transformative contemplative love.

CHAPTER FOUR

Meditating on God in Creation

If the destination of Christian meditation is to live our lives in concert with divine love in our everyday existence, it is fitting that we should begin our practice exploring this destination. For Meister Eckhart there was finally no distinction between looking for God on the inside and looking for God on the outside. In both cases we are seeking to penetrate beneath the surface to discern the divine essence. Meister Eckhart spoke of this truth in these words: "If you fail to seek God and have your eye on him in each and every thing, you will miss this birth" (Fox 1980, 243). St. Bonaventure, a contemporary of Meister Eckhart, lived from 1217 to 1274. He has given us an extraordinary set of spiritual exercises called *The Soul's Journey into God* (Cousins 1978). Bonaventure was minister general of the Franciscan order and professor at the University of Paris. His spiritual exercises, in the spirit of St. Francis, begin with an appreciation for the natural faculties of the human being and with an adoration of God through nature and through the senses.

I begin our practice of Christian meditation with Bonaventure's exercises because they are one of the most practical of the meditation practices we will explore. This practice can be utilized day or night, in a moment's break from work, in the midst of a meeting, and particularly on a few minutes' walk.

I offer this beginning, because it grounds our practice in the world of nature and of things. I think you will also find it a very refreshing complement to the more interior forms of inner healing and meditation that we will explore. If for any reason the other types of interior meditation become difficult or present images that defy understanding or stir fear, please return to this method of meditating on nature. It will ground you and be an excellent companion as you journey through some of the rapids of the purification process. *The Soul's Journey into God* presents a vivid picture of the medieval understanding of the capacities of the human being to stand in relation to all that is. The spiritual exercises begin with an exploration of the human faculties and a wonder and appreciation of them. The seven stages of meditation are given in the chapter titles of the work:

Chapter One: On the Stages of the Ascent into God and on Contemplating Him through His Vestiges in the Universe

Chapter Two: On Contemplating God in His Vestiges in the Sense World

Chapter Three: On Contemplating God through His Image Stamped upon Our Natural Powers

Chapter Four: On Contemplating God in His Image Reformed by the Gifts of Grace

Chapter Five: On Contemplating the Divine Unity through Its Primary Name Which Is Being

Chapter Six: On Contemplating the Most Blessed Trinity in Its Name Which Is Good

Chapter Seven: On Spiritual and Mystical Ecstasy in Which Rest Is Given to Our Intellect When through Ecstasy Our Affection Passes Over Entirely into God.

While I highly recommend the full set of exercises to the curious, I want especially to highlight the first two exercises for our meditation on God in creation. The translator makes a note that the original term used by Bonaventure for "vestiges" is "footprints." I regret that the translation in that particular edition has shied away from the graphic original. The essential exercise we will explore here is "contemplating God through his footprints in the universe." The method will be to "contemplate God through his footprints in the sense world." Our task is simply to pay attention to the ordinary, but with a particular attitude, an attitude of curiosity, of exploration, of revelry in the senses, of delight and of appreciation for the miracle of the created universe.

I suggest the following form to begin to explore this meditation on God in creation. Take a walk, and plan to be out on your walk for twenty to thirty minutes. Walk in nature, if possible, although a city street is also a part of God's creation.

As you walk pay attention to the sounds, sights, smells of your world. Pay attention to the feel of wind and sun, heat or cool, upon your skin. Notice that you receive most of the information about the creation through your senses. Think of the universe you are observing as created by God and that through these forms you can see God's footprints. When you reflect on the nature of the universe, what does it tell you about God? Think of this exercise as a kind of mystery adventure. You've heard all kinds of things about God, you've read all kinds of things. Now it's time to listen to your own experience. When you take in the universe through your senses, what does it tell you about God? Ponder this question when you pause before a tree, a rock, a flower. Take your time and begin your own discoveries of the nature of things.

From time to time, shift your awareness from this grand scheme to be acutely aware of your sensory experience. Really "see." Really "touch." Really "smell." Really "hear." Revel in your senses. Treasure them. Look for the footprints of God in your senses. Again ponder the question for yourself, what does it say about God that we are given these senses for perceiving the creation?

Enjoy!

When you get back from your walk, practice tasting. Enjoy an apple or a cup of tea or coffee. Savor the taste. Appreciate and give thanks for the bounty of creation.

Bonaventure's exercises begin here and I'm sure that is no accident. It is always important to pay attention to beginning places. I take his beginning with the senses and with the creation as also a signal that it is the most fundamental place to do our meditative work. If we get lost within the struggles for making sense out of our lives, it is so important to have a simple way to reconnect with what is essential. I suggest that this exercise is a profound way to reconnect with that which is essential and essentially nourishing for us.

Bonaventure's exercises turn then with some complexity to explore the natural mental faculties in the same way as we have been exploring the senses. If we are created in the image of God, then what does it say of the mystery of God that we possess the qualities of memory, understanding, and will? Bonaventure's meditation turns toward a kind of philosophical speculation, rooted in awe and appreciation of the natural human faculties. Here, I suggest, we find a Western meditative practice correlated with the mindfulness meditations previously described. How would you describe your qualities of mind? From your direct experience of yourself, how would you speak of the nature of God? Bonaventure leads us toward the finding of our own inner truth.

It is only after this venture on our own, into our own perceptions, that he speaks of the gifts of Christ's redemptive work. I suggest that it is at this point that we take up the classical forms of Christian meditation, especially meditation on Scripture and the Jesus Prayer. After we have thoroughly rooted ourselves in what St. Teresa calls the house of self-knowledge, we are ready to be led toward greater wholeness and inner healing.

Bonaventure then turns to the essence of God as perceived in Christian witness, God as Being and God as Good. Here, I suggest, we are in the realm of Centering Prayer, as we shall be exploring it.

Finally, as is almost universally true, the mystic writer leaves off writing in an experience of divine ecstasy. Can you imagine what the world of the senses now looks like to Bonaventure? Perhaps as we move toward our own explorations we shall find out for ourselves.

Often, I suggest returning to the beginning, taking a walk, sitting on a beach or a mountainside, observing nature, reveling in the senses, looking for the footprints of God in creation. If we do no more, we will find our salvation.

CHAPTER FIVE

Meditation on Scripture

Happy are those. . . [whose] delight is in the law of
the Lord, and on [God's] law they meditate day and
night.
They are like trees planted by streams of water,
which yield their fruit in its season, and their leaves
do not wither. In all that they do, they prosper.
(Ps. 1:1-3, NRSV)

At the mid-point of the Christian Scriptures stands this reference to meditating on Scripture. Reflection, meditation,
and prayer over Scripture have been exceedingly important in all of Judeo-Christian history. The Psalms open with
this fascinating description of the fruits of meditation on
the law, the Hebrew Scripture. Those who do shall prosper
in all ways and become like trees planted by a stream, yield-
ing their fruit in due season. The individual who meditates
on Scripture *becomes* the Tree of Life.

In Chapter One, I spoke of the imagery of the Tree of
Life as it appears in the Book of Revelation. There the Tree
of Life is actualized for all creation in the New Heaven and
the New Earth. Here in the Psalms, the Tree of Life is actualized within the individual, as a foretaste of the global
actualization.

We recall that in the mythic structure of Scripture, Adam
and Eve were forbidden to eat of the Tree of Life, which
would have given them full access to the eternal qualities
of life. They have been sent out into the world equipped
only with the knowledge of good and evil, yet with knowledge veiled as to the final realities of God as the eternally
sustaining life force. What has evolved by the imagery of
the Psalms is that the individual believer, immersed in Scripture, may actualize the Tree of Life or the eternity of life
within his or her own being.

Such an image also pervades the teachings of Jesus. "I came that they may have life, and have it abundantly" (John 10:10b, RSV). The quality of life described by Jesus means eternal life, or dwelling in the experience of the eternal creativity of God. Jesus also pointed to the importance of Scripture: "Think not that I have come to abolish the law and the prophets; I have come not to abolish them but to fulfil them. For truly, I say to you, till heaven and earth pass away, not an iota, not a dot, will pass from the law until all is accomplished" (Matt. 5:17-18, RSV). Jesus was himself steeped in Scripture. He demonstrates the truth of Psalm 1: to meditate day and night on the law of the Lord is to become the Tree of Life.

The divine creative expression that brought the world into being, the divine creative expression that operates to sustain nature, is given voice in Scripture. That is the essence of the meaning of Scripture as divinely inspired or as divine revelation. The Hebrew concept of this interface of divine words with divine creative expression is contained in the expression "the *dabhar* of God." *Dabhar* is the "word" of God through which all things have come into being and which is also demonstrated in the words of Scripture. In Greek the term for word is *logos*. The Gospel of John begins with this concept: "In the beginning was the Word, and the Word was with God, and the Word was God. He was in the beginning with God; all things were made through him, and without him was not anything made that was made. In him was life, and the life was the light of [humanity]" (John 1:1-4 RSV). The divine expression has created all that is. In John's Gospel, this creative aspect of God is identified with an eternal Christ, who is already within the heart of all created life and who came in the man Jesus to fully embody the divine hope for human life. The *logos* of John is the *dabhar* of Hebrew thought now personalized in Jesus. In Hebrew thought *dabhar* is not personalized in a person, but in the words of Scripture. The words themselves are ablaze with God.

The mystery of words becomes a doorway to God. A wonderful story out of Jewish tradition illustrates this mysterious possibility. It is the story of a rabbi much respected and loved as a man of God. At the end of his life, he was asked what had been his meditation. He answered, "I started to meditate on Scripture, but I never got past the first word." He had spent his whole life meditating on "In the beginning" or "when things begin." That concept is contained in one Hebrew word, the first word of Scripture. Pause for a moment and think on the mystery of "beginning." Can we not see how rich such a meditation is, how it takes us directly into the essence of life? Such richness hides behind "every word that God utters."

As we begin our meditation on Scripture, it is important to begin with such an attitude of expectancy. It is also important to understand that Scripture reveals its mysteries not by virtue of how many words we study, but by the depth we give to our experience of Scripture. This principle is illustrated in the story of the rabbi. It is also well illustrated by the following story from the Desert Fathers. It is a story that originates among those people who went out into the desert regions of Egypt, Syria, and Palestine in the first three centuries C.E. to seek God in solitude. Many stories are attributed to them. A small collection was made by Thomas Merton in a book entitled *The Wisdom of the Desert* (1960). This story is from Merton's collection.

> Two brethren went to an elder who lived alone in Scete. And the first one said: Father, I have learned all of the Old and New Testaments by heart. The elder said to him: You have filled the air with words. The other one said: I have copied out the Old and New Testaments and have them in my cell. And to this one the elder replied: You have filled your window with parchment. But do you not know Him who said: The kingdom of God is not in words, but in power? And again, Not those who hear the Law will be justified before God but those who carry it out. They asked him, therefore, what was the way of salvation, and he said to them: The beginning of wisdom is the fear of the Lord, and humility with patience. (74)

It is not the quantity of Scripture, but the depth to which we have allowed the divine expression to penetrate into our heart and mind that brings us to saving wholeness. As we begin our practice of meditation on Scripture, an attitude of reverence and simplicity will guide us.

LECTIO DIVINA

As the practice of Christian mysticism has developed through the centuries, the term *lectio divina* has been applied to meditation on Scripture. The term came into common usage by the sixth century, when it was used by St. Benedict in formulating the first rule of monastic life, which became known as the Rule of St. Benedict. From that time onward, the Rule has profoundly shaped Christian life, monastic and non-monastic alike.

The Rule of St. Benedict regulates Christian life according to three practices: *lectio divina*, or study of the divine word (Scripture); *opus dei*, the work of God (worship); and *opus manuum*, work of the hands (manual labor). The day of the monk in the Benedictine tradition has been divided among these three functions. These three functions remain the primary guiding principles of all Christian communities. Christian community does not function well without balanced attention to worship, study, and work.

The practice of *lectio divina* came to be identified with a particular way of approaching Scripture, which is now known as the Benedictine style of meditation (Michael and Norrisey 1984, 31-45). There are four stages to this style of meditation on Scripture. The first step is *lectio*, or reading the Scripture. The second step is *meditatio*, meditating on the passage. The third step is *oratio*, praying on the Scripture. The fourth step, if it comes, is understood as an act of God's grace. It is called *contemplatio*, or contemplation.

This four-fold formula has been elucidated in a twelfth-century text by Guigo II, a Carthusian monk who was Prior at the Grande Chartreuse in France. This small work is a letter that Guigo addressed to a friend, and it is entitled *The Ladder of Monks, a Letter on the Contemplative Life* (1978). Guigo's imagery helps us to understand the flavor of lectio divina practice, and is worthy of somewhat lengthy quotation.

One day when I was busy working with my hands I began to think about our spiritual work, and all at once four stages in spiritual exercise came into my mind: reading, meditation, prayer and contemplation. These make a ladder for monks by which they are lifted up from earth to heaven. It has few rungs, yet its length is immense and wonderful, for its lower end rests upon the earth, but its top pierces the clouds and touches heavenly secrets . . . .

Reading is the careful study of Scriptures, concentrating all one's powers on it. Meditation is the busy application of the mind to seek with the help of one's own reason for knowledge of hidden truth. Prayer is the heart's devoted turning to God to drive away evil and obtain what is good. Contemplation is when the mind is in some sort lifted up to God and held above itself, so that it tastes the joys of everlasting sweetness . . .

Reading seeks for the sweetness of a blessed life, meditation perceives it, prayer asks for it, contemplation tastes it. Reading, as it were, puts food whole into the mouth, meditation chews it and breaks it up, prayer extracts its flavor, contemplation is the sweetness itself which gladdens and refreshes. Reading works on the outside, meditation on the pith: prayer asks for what we long for, contemplation gives us delight in the sweetness which we have found. (81-83)

In his summary, Guigo adds these images:

Reading comes first, and is, as it were, the foundation; it provides the subject matter we must use for meditation. Meditation considers more carefully what is to be sought after; it digs, as it were, for treasure which it finds and reveals, but since it is not in meditation's power to seize upon the treasure, it directs us to prayer. Prayer lifts itself up to God with all its strength, and begs for the treasure it longs for, which is the sweetness of contemplation. Contemplation when it comes rewards the labors of the other three, it inebriates the thirsting soul with the dew of heavenly sweetness. Reading is an exercise of the outward senses; meditation is concerned with the inward understanding; prayer is concerned with desire; contemplation outstrips every faculty. The first degree is proper to beginners, the second to proficients, the third to devotees, the fourth to the blessed. (92-93)

These rich images give us a wonderful sense of the possibilities of *lectio divina* to take us into the heart of God. We begin, as Guigo indicates, with an exercise of the outward senses. We read the Scripture with our eyes. We listen expectantly to the words with our ears. We hope for the revelation that first inspired the words of Scripture to blaze forth again for us. We seek the experience of divine presence hiding in the words of history.

For the actual practice of the meditation phase of *lectio divina*, I suggest that we begin with meditating on a phrase of Scripture. Recall the notion of simplicity of the Desert Fathers. It is not how much of the food of Scripture we lay before ourselves, but how fully we digest it that will be our guiding principle. Thus, we take a phrase, such as "In the beginning, God was creating the heavens and the earth"

(Gen. 1:1). We take that phrase and begin to ponder it. We may adapt it slightly to get to the heart of its meaning. We may also find that even a phrase of this length is too much to consider all at once. So we may meditate upon it in briefer phrases: "In the beginning, God was creating"; "God creates the heavens"; "God creates the earth." There are innumerable ways to "chew" on such a phrase. I suggest adapting the phrase into a few words that you can repeat softly with your inward mind. This is the phase that Guigo describes as the busy application of our own mind to the phrase. This practice is at least initially an exercise of reason

I have found that *lectio divina* meditation on a phrase is an excellent place for us to start our inward Christian meditation practice. It utilizes our rational mind, it utilizes the part of our mind that is always chattering away within us, and it enables us gradually to slow down the speed of the chatter. It cooperates with this verbal function of the mind and begins to turn it toward the mystery of deeper dimensions within ourselves.

As we begin this meditation practice on a phrase of Scripture, I suggest ten to twenty minutes of working with the phrase. What will usually happen is that we will be repeating the phrase inwardly, and at the same time we will notice that associations on the words will begin to surface. Meanings will begin to flow. Sometimes we will find that our mind has wandered quite far from the original phrase. We are partly involved in the training of our ability to stay focused with this practice. Thus, whenever we realize that we have mentally wandered and we are not sure quite how we got to where we are, it is the signal to return to the basics. We return to the phrase and renew our focus on it.

We want an attitude of receptivity and alertness. This attitude can be embodied in our posture. For this type of meditation, I recommend sitting in a chair, with both feet on the floor and with arms and hands balanced in our laps. You may wish to rest your Bible in your lap, so that you can explore different aspects of the phrase. Take the phrase inward, letting your eyes close. Repeat the phrase inwardly, allowing the associations, meanings, and insights to arise. That is the meditation phase of the *lectio divina* practice. You will see that meditation in this way is extremely valuable, and there is no need to move on to the other steps. We would do quite well if we did no more than meditate regularly on the Scripture. So proceed further only as you seem inwardly guided.

The next stage is described as prayer. The Latin term is useful for our understanding of the nature of prayer meant here. *Oratio* means listening and speaking. In *oratio*, we give voice to our deepest longings. For this reason Guigo speaks of prayer as concerned with desire. Guigo's description has taken us into the arena of emotion and relationship. In his description, meditation has aroused in us a sense of the deeper truth of the divine message contained in the Scripture phrase. Now we wrestle with its disclosure in relationship to our own lack of wholeness. Within our meditative prayer experience, we would change our focus at this point from the phrase of Scripture to the life issues that have been raised. Our prayer would involve some aspects of active prayer as discussed earlier. Our prayer would also involve attention to feelings of longing. Our prayer might take the form of inner dialogue with areas of incompleteness. In this respect, the whole therapy session with Tom cited in Chapter Two can be seen as an act of prayer. In meditative prayer periods of twenty minutes to one hour, we will probably find that several of these deeper issues for prayer will surface. We may work with one for a time. Then as it comes to some resolution, I suggest returning to the meditation on the Scripture phrase. Allow your meditation to be the main anchor for your experience, but when deep issues arise, then turn in prayer to them.

Contemplation is described here as a gift. Sometimes it comes and sometimes it does not come. However, for Guigo it is in some ways the driving force behind meditation. It is the dew of heavenly sweetness for which we long. It is the experience of dwelling with God face to face, if for only a few moments. Guigo ends his letter with these words:

> Now it is time for us to end our letter. Let us beseech the Lord together that at this moment He will lighten the load that weighs us down so that we cannot look up to him in contemplation, and in days to come remove it altogether, leading us through these degrees from strength to strength, until we come to look upon the God of gods in Sion, where His chosen enjoy the sweetness of divine contemplation, not drop by drop, not now and then, but in an unceasing flow of delight which no one shall take away, an unchanging peace, the peace of God. (1978, 98-99)

Guigo discovers the direct experience of the celebrative center of life. He experiences the unceasing flow of delight springing from the peace of God.

When the unceasing peace of God comes upon us, our task is to leave aside our longing, to leave aside our pondering, and to enjoy it: to delight inwardly with God. This experience of deep and lasting peace will not come with every meditation experience. From time to time, however, it will come. In those moments, we are invited into the celebrative/creative center of ourselves that is already one with God.

The various terms of the *lectio divina* practice are described as follows:

Stages of *Lectio Divina*

Latin term	English	Faculty	Metaphor
lectio	reading	senses	putting fruit into mouth
meditatio	meditation	reason	chewing the fruit
oratio	prayer	desire	extracting flavor
contemplatio	contemplation	no faculties	delight of sweetness

There are several effective ways to choose the passages of Scripture with which to meditate. One way is to choose a particular book of Scripture that you would like to read. As you read along, perhaps a chapter a day, you will no doubt find that one or two of the key concepts stand out for you. After reading the Scripture, return to those key verses and then allow the meditation phrase to emerge for you.

Another very effective way to meditate on a phrase is to use one phrase for a substantial period. Like the rabbi who meditated on "in the beginning," we find that a phrase of Scripture will reveal numerous levels of meaning if we work with it. We may also find that exactly like the case of the rabbi, one or two words become very important for our meditation. There are no rules here, except to let the Holy Spirit guide us in seeking the revelation of God through the divine word.

I recommend that we also take our scriptural meditation outdoors from time to time. After you have become versed in the practice of focusing on a phrase in an inward way, it is an instructive experience to take a favorite phrase into a walk or other physical exercise. This practice begins to bridge our inner and outer worlds, enabling us to see God in each and every thing.

USING IMAGINATION WITH SCRIPTURE

Another way of meditating on Scripture uses our imagination. This form of meditation has been especially identified with the Spiritual Exercises of St. Ignatius (Mottola 1964). However, the use of imagination with Scripture is not reserved for Ignatius. St. Teresa of Avila also speaks of the use of imagination with Scripture. As these two are contemporaries, we may assume that this practice was in wide use in the sixteenth century.

The technique is simple. The effect can be quite dramatic. We have been exposed to it in the experience of Tom, reported in Chapter Two. Instead of using a phrase for meditation, we take a whole story. It is especially effective to take a story out of the New Testament, particularly the stories of Jesus' healings. We allow our imaginations to build the story in our minds. It is helpful to call in the inner senses as fully as possible. So we seek to listen for the sounds, smell the smells, see colors, textures, buildings, and natural settings, feel the heat or coolness of the day upon our skin. Activating the inner senses brings us fully into the story. We will usually find that the story has a central character who comes to Jesus for healing, or there is a central theme that is at work in the story. In our imagination, we invite ourselves to use the illness or problem of the story as a metaphor for our own areas of need and healing. Thus, we bring ourselves fully into the dynamic of the story. For example, in the stories of paralytics we can ask, how am I paralyzed, emotionally, vocationally, personally? In stories of blindness, we ask how we are spiritually blind, how we are blinded from our divine callings, how we stand in need of insight. In the stories of storms on the sea, we can ask how life is overwhelming us and how we are in need of calm.

One by one, these stories then hold before us the healing, challenging, and calming power of Jesus. In imaginational meditation, Jung's understanding of Christ as a symbol of the Self is activated. Christ comes to represent the potential for wholeness within us. Christ's presence awakens our inner wisdom. Christ is an intermediary to divine healing. The promise of doctrine that Christ stands between humanity and God as the divine force of blessing to us becomes actualized in our own psychic life. We awake to the power and blessing of actualized compassion, which Christ conveys.

For some people, the inner visual imagination is quite acute. For others it is less so. If the first few tries with this form of meditation do not seem fruitful, I suggest that you rest from it a while, continue to develop meditation on a phrase, but return to imagination from time to time. Deep healing can be activated with this form of meditation, whether or not we actually have acute visual imagery. By holding the healing need before the actualized presence of healing in Christ much is accomplished, regardless of whether our inner experience is dramatic or quite subtle.

IMAGERY AND HEALING

To understand more fully the dynamics of healing possible through the use of imagination with Scripture, let us turn to an example. I invite you into the story with which our experience with Tom begins. This guided meditation is based on a story in John 5. After I have guided us through the story, we will conclude our discussion of scriptural meditation with further attention to the dynamics of inner healing.

It is always helpful to begin our Scripture meditation by simply reading the story. I present the story as found in the Revised Standard Version of the Bible.

> After this there was a feast of the Jews, and Jesus went up to Jerusalem.
>
> Now there is in Jerusalem by the Sheep Gate a pool, in Hebrew called Beth-zatha, which has five porticoes. In these lay a multitude of invalids, blind, lame, paralyzed. One man was there, who had been ill for thirty-eight years. When Jesus saw him and knew that he had been lying there a long time, he said to him, "Do you want to be healed?" The sick man answered him, "Sir, I have no man to put me into the pool when the water is troubled, and while I am going another steps down before me." Jesus said to him, "Rise, take up your pallet, and walk." And at once the man was healed, and he took up his pallet and walked. (John 5:1-8)

As we begin to explore this Scripture, it is obvious that we can make best use of it if we understand some of the dynamics within the story by using a biblical commentary. For example, what is the meaning of the part where the man answers Jesus by saying that he has no one to put him into the pool when the water is troubled? People believed that from time to time God would come as a breeze and stir up the water of the pool. When that happened, the first person to get into the pool might be healed as a miracle of God. So this expectation is a primary reason the people have gathered here. With that bit of additional interpretation, let us begin our inner journey with the text.

I would invite you to sit comfortably, with body balanced and open, and with eyes closed. Take a few deep breaths to facilitate relaxation. Let your mind turn to the story. Begin to see Jerusalem, as you would imagine it in Jesus' time, a city on a hill in the distance. Note the colors . . . . In your imagination now enter the city and explore the market place. The Scripture gives us an account that the story takes place at a time of festival. So, we could expect to hear a number of different languages. Listen for these . . . . Notice the sounds of animals and of the buying and selling of the market. Notice the colors and shapes you see. What is the pavement like? Is it dirt and dust, cobblestone, flat stone pavement? Take whatever comes into your own imagination. Notice the excitement and jostling of the crowds as people anticipate the festival taking place . . . .

Now take your imagination to the place in the story, the pool called Beth-zatha. Notice the pool. What is its shape? What is the color of the water? How large is it? . . . Notice the five porticoes . . . . Let your imagination build your own picture of this place . . . .

Now begin to notice the sounds. This is a place of pain and suffering. A place with many lame and ill and blind people. Notice how they interact with one another. Notice how they feel to be in this place where miraculous healings have been reported . . . .

And now begin to notice that you are one of them. You are lying on your pallet, ill for thirty-eight years. How do you feel as this one? (Here we allow our imagination to change the story as needed to accommodate our sex, proceeding as either male or female.) How do you feel being in this place, with these people? . . . In what ways does the ailment of the man in the story reflect your illness? In what ways have you been blind or lame or paralyzed for a very long time? Spend some time with this question before proceeding. Let your own issues begin to surface, using the illness of the story as a metaphor for your diseases of body, mind, or spirit . . . .

In the distance there is movement. A small crowd is approaching, led by a man. As he approaches, allow your imagination to give you your own picture of Jesus. It is not uncommon for people to see Jesus vividly. It is also not uncommon for people to see more of a figure of light without distinct features . . . . Let your own image of Jesus approach. To your surprise he stops before you. He asks, "Do you want to be healed?" Again, take time with this question. This is perhaps the most profound moment of the story. "Do I really want to be released from this habitual problem, from this illness, from this suffering?" In this question, we find our own participation in our infirmities. We find how comfortable we may have become with our not-quite-full life. Or we may desire not to answer directly. Like the man in the story we may find reasons for not being able to find our healing — no one to help me, etc. Search your heart and mind for the proper answer to this question by Jesus: Do you want to be healed?. . .

In the story, after hearing the man's reasons, Jesus simply commands him: "Rise, take up your pallet, and walk." In your imagination, now see yourself arising, being healed of the infirmities you have identified. Imagine yourself set free of them. At least for a moment imagine your new life without your identified infirmities. Feel your body without them. Notice your emotions upon release. Imagine how you will now live your life . . . .

The same type of meditative experience can be created from innumerable Scriptures. Some of the most accessible are: Jesus stilling the sea (Mark 4:33ff.), Jesus healing the man called Legion (Mark 5), Jesus healing the blind man (John 9), Jesus calling forth Lazarus from the tomb (John 11). Morton Kelsey has given a number of guided experiences in this mode as an appendix to *The Other Side of Silence* (1976). As you become versed in the style, it will be quite natural to create your own imaginary ventures into Scripture stories.

What can we surmise about the nature of inner healing from this experience? First it is important to look at the context for healing within Scripture itself. The healings of Jesus take many forms. Sometimes healing is given directly and unsolicited, as in the case of this story. In other cases, Jesus is approached by others on behalf of someone ill. In that context, we are invited to bring our concerns for others into our prayers for healing. In some cases a person approaches with a physical ailment, and Jesus approaches it as a problem of relationship to others, rather than a physical disease. In some cases he asks the petitioner, shall I tell you your sins are forgiven or heal you of your illness? These encounters anticipate the profound implication of our inner attitudes on our physical health that current research is discovering. Finally, there are situations that seem not to be relieved. Paul's mysterious thorn in the flesh is like this. He prays for relief and, finally, after finding none, receives a spiritual solution: the problem will not go away, yet God's grace will sustain him.

Thus, when we approach the crucible of inner healing, I suggest we approach it completely open to outcome. It may be that our dilemma or illness will be answered in the arena in which we are asking for help. It may be that our answer will come from a different arena. It may also be that we must struggle with issues over and over, perhaps even for years before relief comes. However our answers come, I suggest that we also work with the Scripture story fully, taking it to its complete resolution, exploring the metaphorical significance for us of each step in the story.

One of the most compelling factors in healing that comes from scriptural meditation is that it truly calls us into the arena of soul, as we have been describing it. Scripture takes our ego-level questions, problems, and dilemmas and places them in the context of God's eternal creative vision. That perspective alone is often healing. In addition to this grand view, however, the imaginational use of Scripture facilitates intercommunication between the diminished and pained parts of ourselves and the highest wisdom, conveyed in Jesus, as he awakens in our inner experience. When these powers are able to enter into communication with each other, lasting healing is possible. On the model of the soul with which we have been working, subtle and causal energies commune with the repressed and suppressed pains of our earlier life development. To put it more simply, as we stand in the love of God made manifest in the healing presence of Jesus, we are able to tell our own stories of pain and be released from captivity to them.

The stories of Scripture help us to tell our own stories of hidden pain to God and to ourselves. Through this telling, we are able to be released from their captive hold upon us.

CHAPTER SIX

The Jesus Prayer

Lord Jesus Christ, Son of God,
Have mercy on me (a sinner).

HISTORIC ROOTS

The Jesus Prayer has been a mainstay of Eastern Orthodox tradition from the beginning of the Christian era. The Prayer, as presented above, came to the West in the nineteenth century through a Russian writing known as *The Way of a Pilgrim* (French 1952). The work tells of a man's journeys through Russia, accompanied by the Jesus Prayer. On his lips and in his heart and mind is the constant repetition of this prayer.

The collected writings of inner-life development in Orthodox tradition are contained in the *Philokalia* (Kadloubovsky and Palmer 1954). English translations of these writings that date from the fourth to the fifteenth centuries are now available. As described in *The Way of a Pilgrim* (Wakefield 1983, 300), it was an abbreviated Slavic version of these writings, called *Dobrotolubiye*, that the Russian peasant carried for inspiration in his wanderings.

The Jesus Prayer has sometimes been accompanied by a breath awareness. The phrases of the prayer are synchronized with breathing. For example, on breathing in, one may say, "Lord Jesus Christ, Son of God"; and on breathing out, one will say, "Have mercy on me, a sinner." Other breathing variations will use the in breath with "Lord Jesus Christ," out breath with "Son of God"; in breath with "Have mercy on me," out breath with "a sinner." In some versions the last phrase, "a sinner," is left off (A Monk of New Clairvaux 1979, chap. 9).

There have been periods of time when the Jesus Prayer reached out of the monastery and into popular piety. High points of such activity were in fourteenth-century Constantinople and in nineteenth-century Russia. During such periods the prayer has been actively advocated by bishops, as well as taught to visitors to monastic settings.

While the version we have received is lengthy in words and stylized as to content, the earliest versions of the prayer are in the biblical stories of the blind man outside Jericho (Luke 18:38) and of the publican (Luke 18:13). Those texts are simply a cry for mercy.

One of the desert sayings illustrates this simplicity:

One of the fathers told a story of a certain elder who was in his cell busily at work and wearing a hairshirt when Abbot Ammonas came to him. When Abbot Ammonas saw him wearing a hairshirt he said: That thing won't do you a bit of good. The elder said: Three thoughts are troubling me. The first impels me to withdraw somewhere into the wilderness. The second, to seek a foreign land where no one knows me. The third, to wall myself into this cell and see no one and eat only every second day. Abbot Ammonas said to him: none of these three will do you a bit of good. But rather sit in your cell, and eat a little every day, and have always in your heart the words which are read in the Gospel and were said by the Publican, and thus you can be saved. (Merton 1960,41)

Those words are: "Lord, have mercy on me a sinner."

The essence of the Jesus Prayer is this kind of simple prayer, which draws our whole being into the heart. The prayer is often called the Prayer of the Heart. The "heart" in this tradition represents the essential nature of the human being. The intellect may be drawn into the heart through the Jesus Prayer and finally released from speculative activity to a direct perception of divine light. The final destination of the Jesus Prayer is the causal realm, in which speculation ceases and the silent creative essence of God is approached.

The state of tranquility achieved by the practitioners of the Jesus Prayer became known as *hesychasm. Hesychasm* means inward and outward tranquility. It is the peace of God promised by Jesus to his followers: "My peace I give to you; not as the world gives do I give to you" (John 14:27b, RSV). This is the peace that passes understanding; we might more accurately say, the peace that surpasses knowledge or speculation. It is a peace of the heart that transcends the struggles of the intellect. It is an immersion in the essence of the eternal God, from which a peace beyond all the passings of time is given. The *hesychasts* or practitioners of the Jesus Prayer have at times utilized the breath practice with a bowed head to physically enact the drawing of the intellect into the heart. The practice of the prayer has also been reduced simply to the name Jesus. In this form the two syllables have also been synchronized with breath.

As the prayer leads to increasingly subtle inner environments, cautions are generally given to the practitioners. We might say the prayer is at that point for proficients, not for beginners. It is important that we have spent substantial energy on our own purification processes and have substantial sustained experience traversing the ego-Self axis before we jump into the eternal primal radiance. Having stated the concern, however, it also seems to be a fact that purification will naturally oscillate with such times of radiant peace. When those times come, we need to pay attention to them and not use the Jesus Prayer for an escape from the harder questions arising in our awareness. As we pay attention to the whole range of our inner and outer life, we need not be concerned with being too quickly overtaken with the eternal realms. Balance among and attention to all the realms of our lives will serve as a natural grounding to our more subtle inner explorations.

PRAYER ON THE HOLY NAME

In Western Christianity as well as in the Orthodox tradition, there has been a good deal of attention to prayer to Jesus, to Mary, to the Holy Spirit, and to God the Father, in ways that we might call "Prayer on the Holy Name." Scripture itself abounds with references to praying through the name of Jesus. Jesus' own formula for prayer in the Lord's Prayer uses the name of God in a similar vein.

In the Prayer on the Holy Name, we have the name given and then a petition. We call ourselves to awareness of the divine through the form of the divine name, and then we give our human response. The Jesus Prayer follows this form:

divine name	*human response*
Lord Jesus Christ,	
son of God,	have mercy on me, a sinner.

We see the same form in the beginning of the Lord's Prayer:

divine name *human response*
Our Father,
who art in heaven, hallowed be Thy name.

A similar form is present in ascriptions to Mary:

divine name *human response*
Hail Mary,
full of grace, the Lord is with you.

There are also ascriptions to the Holy Spirit:

divine name *human response*
Come, Holy Spirit,
come, fill the hearts of your faithful.

In this light, and in light of the numerous historic variations on the Jesus Prayer, it is quite appropriate for us to work with the words of the Jesus Prayer to devise a form that speaks most directly to our current needs. The Jesus Prayer thus becomes a direct expression of our own personal needs and celebrations in the moment. Ron DelBene has utilized this liberty with great benefit in his work with breath prayer (DelBene and Montgomery 1981). DelBene has the individual invite God to ask us, what do you need or want? In answering the question, we get the response side of the prayer. Then we direct it to the form or name of God that is most meaningful to us at the time. Thus we create a prayer phrase like: Jesus, sustain me; Father, have mercy; or Lord Jesus, heal me.

As I have worked with the Jesus Prayer with people through the years, I have been struck with the benefit of praying it both in its classical form and also using spontaneous prayers on the Holy Name. Not uncommonly an individual will initially have resistance to the full formula of the Jesus Prayer. It will seem cumbersome or even antithetical to some of their life-experiences and beliefs. Some people see it as a subservient prayer. Some have difficulty saying "a sinner." The phrase conveys full historical tradition, and thus also presents to us any difficulties we may have with much of the Christian tradition, particularly its doctrines of sin and grace. For this reason, I have suggested that people use an adapted form if that is more meaningful. What is also not uncommon is that a few years into a regular meditation life, people find that the historic form of the Jesus Prayer is alive for them. Even those who had difficulty earlier have somehow gained a humility that allows for a new understanding of the need for grace and the acknowledgment of sin that the Jesus Prayer states.

I encourage you to test your own experience and to explore the Jesus Prayer in its historic form and in forms you will adapt to your own use.

WHO IS THIS CHRIST?

The use of the Jesus Prayer draws us directly into the deepest questions of Christian life, the questions that surrounded Jesus in his historical life, the questions that led to the formulation of the church's doctrine, the questions that have led to schisms and heresies, the questions of faith that each of us must finally answer alone. Who is this Christ? What is the nature of the eternal creative energy presented to us in the life of Jesus, the energy that comes forth as the direct divine expression, made visible in Jesus? Is this eternal radiant light the Christ? Is Christ the dying crucified one? Or both? Is the Christ in the guise of a man for me, or an energy I feel but cannot describe? Who is this Christ? What does the cosmic Christ of contemporary teachings have to do with the Jesus of Scripture? Finally, we must ask the real question behind all the other questions: Can I be redeemed from my eternal struggles by relating to this Jesus Christ, or should I look to another avenue for salvation?

Those are a few of the questions of faith the use of the Jesus Prayer raises. They are not new questions. They are some of the most profound questions of Christian life. They are some of the questions that were on the mind of the followers of Jesus and the ones who did not follow him. They were questions in the minds of the writers of the gospels. They were the questions on the hearts of the spurned Gnostics. They were the questions that Paul answered in his writings. They are the questions that haunt us as Western people, whether or not we address them consciously. Jesus Christ stands in the forefront of the Western psyche. He is the archetypal expression of the highest human potential for the West. He is the essential *someone* in our mystic community with whom we must come to terms.

What can we learn of his essence from our emerging transpersonal model of human consciousness? Can this model of consciousness help us in our time to relate to the challenge of these historic questions? Let us look at this understanding from the perspective of God, as presented in the model. From this perspective God is the ground and source of all that is. God is thus no-thing. God is beyond things; God is the eternally creating essence from which all things spring. God is also the eternal living essence within all things. God is the life-force. God is "creating." God is that which creates, without which nothing is.

If God is that eternal essence within all things, then the witness of Christian faith, the essential witness of Jesus is that this essence is not aloof. This essence is accessible. We can personally relate to and thus know this essence. Furthermore to be in such relationship with the eternal essence of the creating God is to taste salvation or healing wholeness. It is to be released from the bonds of sin and death. If we understand the bonds of sin to be the bonds of self-imposed and other-imposed limits to the creative expression of life, we do indeed "dwell" in sin. Our current socio-political systems perpetuate sin and are also the arena of redemption, as we allow creative energy to flow into them, as we cooperate with the divine creative essence in creating new forms of social life. In the personal arena, we are also delivered from the bonds of sin. Jesus included our inner struggles as an arena of sin. Sin is being disconnected from our own essential creativity, from the divine source within us, the eternal God who is the essence of our life. To be redeemed is to "know" this source, this inner force directly. This inner force has been called the indwelling God or the Holy Spirit by some; by others it is called the inner Christ, God made visible. To directly know or perceive or live in constant relationship to this essence is also to overcome the barrier of death. This divine eternal essence that is the ground of our being in physical life is the ground and essence of our personality and of all life forms. Thus, there is a corrective that this understanding offers to our emerging model of consciousness. God is not only the essence of life that we meet at our center in and beyond the causal realm and at the outer bounds of the world; God made visible or the Christ-Spirit is also to be found as the ground of each discrete level of consciousness and of community. Figure 6 illustrates this concept. To speak of God as eternal or as no-thing means that God is also the essence of all things. Whatever can be described and named, be it a style of consciousness like rational-ego or a thing of nature like a tree, has at its essence the "is-ness" of God. That is the essential witness of Jesus Christ. God is literally at the heart of all that is, and God is good, indeed, more than good, God is beneficent. This creative essence is *actively* seeking good for all creatures. The Gospel of John identifies the beneficent activity of God as the *logos*, the Christ. Divine beneficence *is* the cosmic Christ at every level of being.

From this emerging model we also discover that we would perceive God uniquely in each level of consciousness and community. To outline some of the ways God is revealed as ground essence of these different levels carries with it the risk of sounding reductionist. God is much more than can be said in a few words or perceived through a single slant on any perspective. In the arena of ego, God is the ground of human personality and uniqueness. Thus, the Christian doctrine of the "resurrection of the body" has meant not simply body, but unique personality. The Christian perspective is that personality is sacred, each person a unique expression of divine essence. Ego in Christianity thus becomes not something to be lost, but something to be redeemed and brought into union and creative co-creation with God. In the arena of reason, God is discovered in acts of creative problem solving, in the tasks of approaching the problems and questions of life. God, we might say, is thus also the source of the scientific method of inquiry, through which new technologies for enhancing and destroying life are discovered. God in the imaginal/feeling realm is the healing enacted in psychotherapy, in dreams, in stories of mythology and Scripture. Here God is the healing power of story to release us from victimization by our own psychological complexes. In the realm of body/ego and body/mind integration, God is the essence of the body recreating itself and renewing itself. Here God is the essence of the biological, cellular creative process. At the subtle level, God is presented as an inner vision of Jesus or Mary or other spiritual wisdom figure. The subtle realm is thus the starting point of the Jesus Prayer. Here is the arena of God as found in the healing presence of the inner Jesus Christ. In causal realm experience, we experience God as radiant light, or beneficent dark, as the least formed, yet still describable approximation of Essence. In our inner meditation, this is the realm where the Jesus Prayer takes us into the experience of peace, or *hesychasm*, as even the subtle form of the figure of Jesus merges with our own personality into one "is-ness" of God.

God—Divine Ground of Being

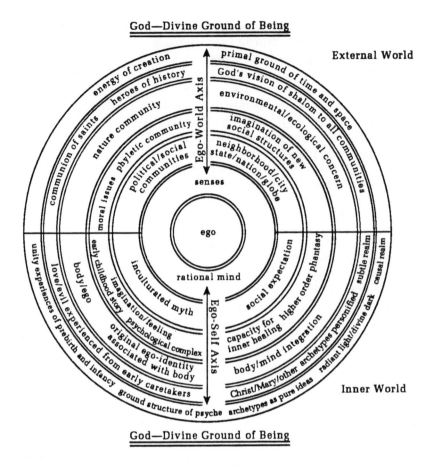

Figure 6
(Adapted from Wilber, 1980)

In the world, we see these essences as well. God is the ground of our sensory experience and the source of pleasure in the senses. God is the source and ground of all social orders and the struggle for justice and peace. In our phyletic community we encounter God as intimacy and the surrounding of love that is possible in forgiven and affirming relationships. In nature, God is the mystery of creation. The subtle and causal realms we experience through the outward journey into the world merge with the subtle and causal realms of the interior world. Thus, we see God active in history as its compelling force toward freedom. And we see God as the primal ground of time and space. Christ may be understood as the guiding force toward wholeness within each level of experience, the bridge between current reality and the divine creative potential.

All this suggests that there are many ways in which we encounter Christ in our experience. Much will have to do with our own "callings" toward the different levels of experience in our model. Much will have to do with our own stage of life and whether, for example, the press of family, aging parents or young children is upon us. Much will have to do with our proclivities of personality toward experiencing life primarily through our reason, imagination, or senses. But the witness of Jesus Christ is that the saving relationship with God as creative divine beneficence is available to us in all circumstances of life and in all arenas of consciousness and that Jesus Christ provides guidance toward that beneficence.

The essence of the doctrine of the Incarnation is that God becomes born "flesh of flesh." God takes on the form of an individual human being. This act is "saving" to humanity. The name Jesus means, "he shall save his people from their sins" (Matt. 1:21). In other ascriptions, he is called "Emmanuel," meaning, "God is with us" (Matt. 1:23). He is called "Messiah," the Hebrew term for the savior, the one who will deliver the whole social order from political disorder (Luke 2:11). He is called "Son of God" (Luke 1:35). "Christ" is the Greek term for Messiah, the anointed one or Son of God.

The great question of Scripture is whether or not Jesus as historical person is really the Christ. John the Baptist sends emissaries to ask Jesus if he is the Christ, and Jesus answers, "the blind receive their sight and the lame walk, lepers are cleansed and the deaf hear, and the dead are raised up, and the poor have good news preached to them. And blessed is [the one] who takes no offense at me" (Matt. 11:5-6, RSV). To be in the company of Jesus is to be in the experience of divine benevolent creativity. The whole tradition of Jesus' healing ministry points toward an extraordinary embodiment of divine power within the man Jesus. And in his crucifixion we witness the transformation of our personal relationship to death and the transformation of evil within the historical/political order. Thus we may see the whole of the scriptural witness to Jesus to say that the divine beneficence permeates all flesh, all things, all forms. And at the same time, we are blind and ignorant of that essence and must be brought into relationship with that essence. Jesus saves us when we discover through his life, his teachings, his death and resurrection that "God is with us." This teaching is the fundamental perspective of the Gospel of John:

> In the beginning was the Word, and the Word was with God, and the Word was God. He was in the beginning with God; all things were made through him, and without him was not anything made that was made. In him was life, and the life was the light of [humanity]. The light shines in the darkness, and the darkness has not overcome it.... The true light that enlightens every man [and woman] was coming into the world. He was in the world, and the world was made through him, yet the world knew him not. He came to his own home, and his own people received him not. But to all who received him, who believed in his name, he gave power to become children of God; who were born, not of blood nor of the will of the flesh nor of [human] . . . will . . . , but of God. (John 1:1-5, 9-12 RSV)

What then shall we say of evil, or of the drive toward destruction within human life, or of the casual slaughter by nature of itself? The interpretation we have been developing here points toward evil as a product of ignorance. Because each of the entities of creation have a degree of freedom and they act in their own seeming self-interest, pain and suffering are inflicted by creature upon creature. Furthermore, because each of the social levels we have been describing also has its own "life," then the accumulated suffering of individuals when systematized within a social structure creates a higher degree of suffering. All these levels of suffering are addressed in Paul's notion of the creation groaning as if in the pangs of childbirth (Romans 8). Evil, as suffering inflicted by one creature upon another, seems inherent in the present order of creation. But the drive toward the *shalom* of God spurs us toward the alleviation of that suffering wherever we bring it to consciousness. At this point in our evolution, such concern may manifest as a desire to alleviate pain in the killing of animals for food. At some point, it may mean the release of humanity from inflicting death on animals for our sustenance. At present it means concern, indeed anguish, over the destruction of forests. In the future it may mean that we will understand how to cooperate with nature, while sustaining our massive global human population. To pray for salvation through Jesus Christ is to open ourselves to all levels of the suffering that earthly life endures and to enter into the possibility of deliverance through the divine beneficent creativity. Thus, each of us in our own prayer becomes the doorway through which God can again become Emmanuel, manifest as the creative idea, the creative act that is saving to God's own world.

We can ask who Christ is, in a meaningful way, only if we ask in the context of our potential as humans to be intermediary beings, the ones who stand in relationship to all other creatures. When we approach Christ, with the affirmation of "Emmanuel," "God is with us," then each of us becomes the doorway through which God can be born as saving idea and as saving action to a suffering world. In each of our hearts and minds and bodies, God wants to be remembered and thus given power to transform and unify life further. All this and much more we mean when we approach Jesus Christ in our inner prayer and in the outward world.

The spirit of *hesychasm* and the spirit of constant prayer are the same spirit. It is the spirit of seeing God in everything. It is the spirit of discerning Emmanuel everywhere. It is the spirit of discovering the meaning of Christ described by the Gospel of John as the Spirit that enlivens everything that is. Thus, we are also brought to the discovery of the Russian peasant in *The Way of a Pilgrim*, that the Jesus Prayer is to be prayed always and everywhere. This constant prayer enables us to commune with the divine everywhere, in the innermost recesses of our own minds and hearts and in the demands of social and political life. We are after nothing less than the complete transformation of our inner and outer worlds into *shalom*.

REDEEMING YOUR RELATIONSHIP WITH JESUS CHRIST

There is no area fraught with more challenge for Westerners than our relationship with Jesus Christ. Whether we consider ourselves within the boundaries of the church or outside those boundaries, there is much unfinished business for many of us around this historical and cosmic figure. When I have introduced the Jesus Prayer in settings of clergy and laity, as well as in settings of persons disenchanted with Christianity, I have learned to expect this prayer to elicit a good deal of difficulty for some individuals. Because of injury the church and its exponents have caused us, or perhaps because we have not developed our thinking on Jesus Christ since childhood or adolescence, we will find resistance to praying through Jesus.

An important step in liberating our thinking about Jesus Christ is to realize that there are many aspects to Jesus. At different times of our life one or another of these aspects will be more important. I would say, from my own experience and from my experience with others, that Jesus Christ is the primary symbol of the Self for Westerners. He does embody the wholeness to which we aspire, wholeness of external and internal relationships, as well as wholeness of embodiment of God in human flesh. That he is male presents problems to women and men alike. That his message is obscured in historical Scriptures presents other difficulties. Nevertheless, even within these confines there are numerous aspects of his embodiment of the Self that can speak to us. If Christ is the symbol of the Self, then these different aspects are like the garments the Self wears to speak to us with clarity and challenge at different times. To begin to redeem this powerful symbol of the Self, this powerful bridge into our divine essence, I would like to enumerate some of the various "garments" Jesus wears in Scripture and tradition.

Jesus is first of all infant in Scripture. Can we relate to Jesus as baby, as the potentiality contained in the infant, and as the one in need of our own nurturing to bring to fullness of life? It has been reported that the great Christian thinker Pierre Teilhard de Chardin used Jesus as infant as his life-long meditation.

There is Jesus as growing youth, attaining knowledge, understanding, strength, and vision. It may have been many years since we thought of this aspect of Jesus. Jesus, the youth teaching in the Temple, may have inspired us in our childhood and adolescence. What would it mean in middle age, in old age, to relate again to Jesus as youth? We may gain great vision and endurance from returning to the vigor of youth through meditation on Jesus as a youth.

There is Jesus the teacher. Here is an aspect to which many people relate in our times. Whether or not one can make sense of the miracles or of the crucifixion or of other dynamics in the traditions of Jesus, his teachings may be admired and appreciated. To relate more effectively to Jesus the teacher, we may study his teaching parables and stories again. We may cultivate him within our own inner experience as a source of personal guidance and wisdom.

Jesus also appears as the healer. The healing stories, especially encountered in imaginative meditation, can come alive and awaken the inner Christ as a center of powerful love and radiant healing within us. We can learn to call upon Jesus the healer to be with us in situations in which we are asked to pray for healing of others. The simplest and perhaps most powerful traditions of healing prayer simply involve placing one's hands on a suffering person, inviting the healing Jesus to be present through us and praying for the other.

Jesus is also manifest as an individual of prayer, with a life of interior struggle. One of the most revealing lines of Scripture occurs immediately after Jesus is baptized and has received the blessing of God. "Thereupon the Spirit sent him away into the wilderness, and there he remained for forty days tempted by Satan. He was among the wild beasts; and the angels waited on him" (Mark 1:12-13, NEB). Jesus was no stranger to the questions of the soul. Here we may find him to be companion and friend to our own struggles for authenticity before God. Time and again, he withdraws for prayer, to struggle through the difficult decisions confronting him. He is a consummate example of the interior life.

Jesus is shown to be friend and companion, weeping over the death of his friend, Lazarus, and responding out of friendship to Mary and Martha.

We also encounter Jesus as social liberator overturning the tables of the moneychangers in the Temple. He reaches out to the social outcasts of his time. His challenge to us is inescapable: as you have fed the hungry, clothed the naked, visited the imprisoned, you have done it unto me.

Jesus is the crucified one, faithful to God unto death. He is the one who has suffered as we have suffered, who shares our griefs and bears our sorrows. He can give mercy freely because he has been in the excruciating places of human suffering.

Jesus is the resurrected one who overcomes the barriers of death, who descends into hell, who redeems us even beyond the confines of human life and death. He is the gateway for us into the eternal aspect of God.

Finally, he is viewed also as Lord of history. In the Book of Revelation, Jesus comes from beyond his own historical epoch with the sword of truth to challenge and redeem us regardless of our time in the history of earthly life.

What is missing in Scripture is Jesus as intimate, as lover, as spouse. We see him as loyal member of his family, as son caring for his mother from the cross, but we do not see him as intimate. This deficiency has been corrected in mystical tradition, where Jesus has been viewed as lover and spouse. St. Teresa writes: "Speak with Him as with a father, or a brother, or a lord, or as with a spouse; sometimes in one way, at other times in another; He will teach you what you must do in order to please him" (Kavanaugh and Rodriguez 1980, 141). Her imagery of divine union in the *Interior Castle* uses the language of engagement, betrothal, and marriage (ibid., 335-452). There have been instances of men using this imagery with Jesus as well, for example, in the rhapsodic devotional descriptions of Charles Wesley (1707-88):

> Jesus, lover of my soul,
> Let me to thy bosom fly,
> While the nearer waters roll,
> While the tempest still is high:
> Hide me, O my Savior, hide, till
> the storm of life is past;
> Safe into the haven guide;
> O receive my soul at last!

> (1989)

Thus, when we approach Jesus, we do approach a multifaceted figure, capable of relating to us in whatever way is most beneficial. As we approach our practice of the Jesus Prayer, that is a principle that will guide us.

PRACTICING THE JESUS PRAYER

As you begin to practice the Jesus Prayer, I suggest that you spend some time with the historical form, discovering whether it speaks directly to you or if it poses too many difficulties to be useful. After all, the purpose of this prayer is to enter into transforming union with God. If the form of the prayer itself poses too much mental static for us, it is not contributing to our discovery of *hesychasm*, but distracting us. Try it, however, for yourself, turning over the phrases in your heart and mind, "Lord Jesus Christ, Son of God, have mercy on me, a sinner." Synchronize your breath with the phrase. Invite your imagination to give you an image of Jesus Christ. Allow that image to stand or sit before you. Allow yourself at times to merge with Christ. Allow the Jesus Prayer to take you face to face with divine creative essence. At times practice it in the eyes-closed, sitting posture. At other times, take a walk with the Jesus Prayer, or use it with other forms of exercise. Notice what a difference it makes to view your world through the perspective of looking for Christ in each and every thing.

To devise your own variation of the Jesus Prayer, simply look for that image of Jesus most meaningful to you. So, it might mean that your prayer phrase would not focus on Jesus as "Lord," but rather as brother, friend, spouse, lover, social reformer, healer, teacher, youth, or any other of the rich relationships we have been exploring. Once when I was teaching the prayer, a seminary student expressed the struggle he was having with his relationship with Christ. I asked him to think about what held symbolic meaning for him. He thought for a while and responded that water was a powerful symbol for him. Then after a while longer, he expressed the following prayer phrase: "Christ, the living water, flow through me." The heart of the Jesus Prayer is that we find that expression that most directly brings us into relationship with the divine essence.

Finally, if we find that the male image of Jesus is too distracting or not fulfilling, we may recall the rich tradition of devotion to Mary within Roman Catholic and Eastern Orthodox tradition. In Eastern Orthodox tradition, Mary is understood as *theotokos*, the "Mother of God." What an astonishing and liberating meditation: humanity is the form through which God comes to birth. The Gnostic tradition developed a devotional life to Mary Magdalene as well. We may take our own leads from our interior and develop the "Prayer on the Holy Name" in a way that guides us into the celebrative center of divine creation.

Lord Jesus Christ, Son of God,
have mercy on me, a sinner.

We are led back to the affirmation of the historical formulation. The human conditions of sin and suffering can be overcome, grace can abound. God can be experienced face to face. A seventh century text of the *Philokalia* speaks of the types of inner experience we may find with the Jesus Prayer. St. Maximus the Confessor (d. 655) writes:

The highest state of pure prayer has two forms.... The sign of the first order is when a man collects his mind, freeing it of all worldly thoughts, and prays without distraction and disturbance, as if God Himself were present before him, as indeed He is. The sign of the second is when, in the very act of rising in prayer, the mind is ravished by the Divine boundless light and loses all sensation of itself or of any other creature, and is aware of Him alone, Who, through love, has produced in him this illumination. In this state, moved to understand words about God, he receives pure and luminous knowledge of him (Kadloubovsky and Palmer 1954, 299-300).

With the Jesus Prayer, or Prayer on the Holy Name, we begin with God before us, in the form of Jesus or Mary or the Holy Spirit. Then in the midst of the prayer, we may find we are simply led beyond form into the "divine boundless light." If this state of grace comes, our task is to receive and experience the silent refreshment of God. If it does not come, we realize that God may have other arenas where our attention is needed. And in all our prayer and meditation, we offer ourselves to be utilized for God's new birth. In each act of prayer, we repeatedly become the "Mother" of God.

CHAPTER SEVEN

Centering Prayer

The Cloud of Unknowing (Johnston 1973) is a fourteenth-century text by an anonymous English author. It is one of the classics of Western contemplative literature, a book especially written for people engaged in the work of *apophatic* contemplation. The term *apophatic* means without image. The other types of meditation we have been exploring would be broadly characterized as *kataphatic*, or meditation with image. *The Cloud of Unknowing* addresses the contemplation stage of the four-stage *lectio divina* practice. It also addresses the stage of the Jesus Prayer, where we are swept up into the divine boundless light. It is especially written for advanced meditators. However, in the foreword to the text, the following invitation is given to any who are drawn toward a more loving life:

> There are some presently engaged in the active life who are being prepared by grace to grasp the message of this book. I am thinking of those who feel the mysterious action of the Spirit in their inmost being stirring them to love. I do not say that they continually feel this stirring, as experienced contemplatives do, but now and again they taste something of contemplative love in the very core of their being. Should such folk read this book, I believe they will be greatly encouraged and reassured. (44)

Indeed, the essence of *The Cloud of Unknowing* is contained in one sentence: "The contemplative work of love by itself will eventually heal you of all the roots of sin" (4). This statement takes us into the heart of the contemplative practice of the text. It invites us all, whether proficient contemplatives or not, to discover its meaning in our inner and outward lives. The practice of contemplation as described in *The Cloud of Unknowing* has been popularized recently by Fr. Thomas Keating, Fr. Basil Pennington, and others. The term for the prayer that is used in this new teaching is "Centering Prayer" (Pennington 1980). For convenience, I will use that term as we explore the practice.

PRINCIPLES OF CENTERING PRAYER

The key understanding on which Centering Prayer is based is the distinction between knowing and loving. *The Cloud of Unknowing* expresses the principle this way:

> Try to understand this point. Rational creatures such as [people] and angels possess two principal faculties, a knowing power and a loving power. No one can fully comprehend the uncreated God with his knowledge; but each one, in a different way, can grasp [God] fully through love. Truly this is the unending miracle of love: that one loving person, through . . . love can embrace God, whose being fills and transcends the entire creation. And this marvelous work of love goes on forever, for [the One] whom we love is eternal. Whoever has the grace to appreciate the truth of what I am saying, . . . take my words to heart, for to experience this love is the joy of eternal life while to lose it is eternal torment. (50)

In Centering Prayer we approach God beyond form, we approach God directly as ground essence, the creative potentiality of all things, the One who is no-thing. We approach an arena beyond knowledge. For the author of *The Cloud of Unknowing*, this divine ground can be comprehended through love, not through knowledge.

Centering Prayer is thus a work of the heart, and a work essentially of feeling. At the most subtle of levels the work of contemplative love in the individual transforms all motivations into love. Without singling out our various motivations and scrutinizing them to root out our destructive and life-negating habits of thought and emotion, Centering Prayer places all of them before the power of love. This contemplative love is a "power." It is a felt force, an energy that transforms all it touches. We might say that it is the divine beneficence coming forth from where it dwells within us to bathe everything we can imagine or feel or think or encounter with its blessing. Contemplative love heals us from all the roots of sin because it overcomes all alienations. It places everything into the essential, compassionate benevolence of God. It overwhelms our sin with blessing.

For the author, this inner work of love leads also to outward reconciliation.

> The work of love not only heals the roots of sin, but nurtures practical goodness. When it is authentic you will be sensitive to every need and respond with a generosity unspoiled by selfish intent. Anything you attempt to do without this love will certainty be imperfect, for it is sure to be marred by ulterior motives. Genuine goodness is a matter of habitually acting and responding appropriately in each situation, as it arises, moved always by the desire to please God. [God] alone is the pure source of all goodness and if a person is motivated by something else besides God, even though God is first, then his virtue is imperfect. This is evident in the case of two virtues in particular, humility and brotherly love. Whoever acquires these habits of mind and manner needs no others, for [that person] will possess everything. (64)

While the practice of contemplative love is identified with a particular method of interior prayer, its effects linger long afterward. We are encouraged to practice contemplative love as a form of constant prayer in all our relationships and in every waking moment.

What is the contemplative practice described as Centering Prayer? The author speaks of this practice as an advanced meditation practice. His directive is that we constantly turn our attention from the mental arena to that of a "naked" attitude of love. His point is that we will not directly experience God or contemplative love only by thinking about it. Furthermore, the intellect has the power to argue forever over this point or that. So, even in thinking on so good a thing as God, the intellect will keep us finally away from the direct experience of God. All this activity he calls intellectualizing. The author assumes that we have each done our portion of this kind of intellectual work before we turn to Centering Prayer. That is why the practice is called an advanced practice. "Anyone who expects to advance without having meditated often on [one's] own sinfulness, the Passion of Christ, and the kindness, goodness, and dignity of God, will most certainly go astray and fail in [this] purpose" (56). It is thus very appropriate that we approach Centering Prayer last in our discussion of Christian meditation practices. As we have learned to meditate on Scripture, as we have pondered our own conditions of illness and disease in the imaginal use of Scripture, as we have explored our relationship with Christ in the Jesus Prayer, we have laid the foundation for Centering Prayer practice.

The author continues with these instructions:

> But a person who has long pondered these things must eventually leave them behind beneath a *cloud of forgetting* if [that one] hopes to pierce the *cloud of unknowing* that lies between [us] and [our] God. So whenever you feel drawn by grace to the contemplative work and are determined to do it, simply raise your heart to God with a gentle stirring of love. Think only of God, the God who created you, redeemed you, and guided you to this work. Allow no other ideas about God to enter your mind. Yet even this is too much. A naked intent toward God, the desire for [God] alone, is enough.
>
> If you want to gather all your desire into one simple word that the mind can easily retain, choose a short word rather than a long one. A one-syllable word such as 'God' or 'love' is best. But choose one that is meaningful to you. Then fix it in your mind so that it will remain there come what may. This word will be your defense in conflict and in peace. Use it to beat upon the cloud of darkness above you and to subdue all distractions, consigning them to the *cloud of forgetting* beneath you. Should some thought go on annoying you demanding to know what you are doing, answer with this one word alone. If your mind begins to intellectualize over the meaning and connotations of this little word, remind yourself that its value lies in its simplicity. Do this and I assure you these thoughts will vanish. Why? Because you have refused to develop them with arguing (56).

The imagery of the two clouds is designed simply as a tool for beginning our contemplative work. In another place in the text, the author is very clear that any references to God that would indicate that God is somewhere more than anywhere else is inaccurate. God is not up or down. So, the clouds here are not meant to convey that God is more above than below or outside than inside us. But they do enable us to begin very nicely to participate in the healing dynamics of contemplative love. The cloud of unknowing also contains a rich scriptural meaning.

The cloud of unknowing is the cloud of revelation. At key moments in Scripture, when God gives revelation, it is within a cloud. On Mt. Sinai, Moses is hidden in a cloud as God reveals the law. On the Mount of Transfiguration, Jesus is surrounded by a cloud as God reveals his lineage and companionship with Moses and Elijah. This rich image of the cloud as the mysterious place of revelation is the context for the practice of Centering Prayer.

The cloud of forgetting is a tool to enable our minds to learn "letting go." Whenever we find thoughts stirring us into quarrelling, distracting us from the spirit of contemplative love, we answer them with the one word we have chosen for the meditation and release them into the cloud of forgetting. The cloud of forgetting is simply the other side of the cloud of unknowing. The author's intent is that we learn to "dwell" in contemplative love, that our attention become wholly absorbed in the experience of naked desire or love of God. His position is that anything we can think of, anything we can imagine, is less than God. Thus, we will finally be brought before God through the feeling of love and nothing else. The cloud of forgetting is a convenient metaphor for this desire to release all else from our awareness except the "naked intent toward God, the desire for [God] alone."

As I have read and practiced this text, it seems clear to me that the author also uses the one-word meditation as a tool. If one needs it to remain focused in contemplative love, one may choose a word. If one can keep one's attention absorbed in the loving power, a word is not necessary. As you practice Centering Prayer, I suggest that you begin with a word. From time to time you may find the feeling quality of contemplative love will be strong enough that you can even let go of the word. I think that is in the spirit of the author's suggestions.

Note the gentleness of these instructions. Find a word that you like, preferably a one-syllable word such as "God" or "love." "But choose one that is meaningful to you." As we begin our Centering Prayer practice, choose a word, one word or a very short phrase, a word or phrase that reminds you of the creative/celebrative center that is God in your own essence and at the essence of all that is. Then, *whatever comes to mind, answer it with this word and with the spirit of contemplative love.* That instruction is the single most reconciling statement I have found in all of spiritual and psychological literature. Allowing anything to come to mind and answering it with "God," "love," or our own life-giving word is the work of contemplative love healing us of the roots of sin. I invite you into the divine healing presence of this power called contemplative love.

Thus, when we begin Centering Prayer, we will usually be sitting or lying down, with eyes closed. Imagine that beneath you is the cloud of forgetting. Practice using the cloud of forgetting by letting go of tensions in your body. Practice using the cloud of forgetting by letting go of the tasks of the day and by bringing yourself present to this moment of prayer. Imagine that you are surrounded by the cloud of unknowing, that this cloud interpenetrates your body, heart, mind, and soul. Acknowledge the limits of your knowledge and the final mystery of God and of life that this cloud represents. Allow yourself to await with anticipation what God may reveal to you today in this cloud. Then stir up the feeling of love in your heart, the desire to know God, your naked loving intent to be joined in communion with God. Let your whole being, your whole consciousness, be absorbed in this loving, longing feeling. Allow a single word or a very short phrase to emerge that will help you stay in awareness of contemplative love. Let this word be repeated gently, slowly, with your inner voice. Begin the work of contemplative love. Whatever comes to mind, answer it with this word and with the spirit of loving desire for God and then, as you are able, let it go into the cloud of forgetting. "Let your longing relentlessly beat upon the cloud of unknowing that lies between you and your God. Pierce that cloud with the keen shaft of your love..." (63).

Be alert in the practice of Centering Prayer for the possibility of "God's action, which is the awakening of love and which [God] alone can do" (83).

> Then perhaps [God] may touch you with a ray of . . . divine light which will pierce the *cloud of unknowing* between you and [your God]. [God] will let you glimpse something of the ineffable secrets of . . . divine wisdom and your affection will seem on fire with [divine] love. I am at a loss to say more, for the experience is beyond words (84).

The practice of Centering Prayer leads us into the heart of God, which is the ineffable experience of love. We are reminded of Dante's experience of God as the "primal love" or St. Maximus's experience of the "divine boundless light."

THE TRANSFORMATIVE WORK OF CENTERING PRAYER

As we look at the effects of the practice of Centering Prayer upon our lives, we would remember that it is from this author that we have one of the most powerful descriptions of the dignity of human life in medieval literature.

> Beneath you and external to you lies the entire created universe. Yes, even the sun, the moon, and the stars. They are fixed above you, splendid in the firmament, yet they cannot compare to your exalted dignity as a human being. The angels and the souls of the just are superior to you inasmuch as they are confirmed in grace and glorious with every virtue, but they are your equals in nature as intelligent creatures. By nature you are gifted with three marvelous spiritual faculties, Mind, Reason, and Will, and two secondary faculties, Imagination and Feeling. There is nothing above you in nature except God . . . . When you are reading books about the interior life and come across any references to yourself, understand it to mean your whole self as a human being of spiritual dignity and not merely your physical body. As [a person] you are related to everything in creation through the medium of your faculties. If you understand all this about the hierarchy of creation and your own nature and place in it, you will have some criteria for evaluating the importance of each of your relationships. (129)

Thus, for the author of *The Cloud of Unknowing*, the work of contemplative love within one individual extends through that individual to the entire created universe. Through the spiritual faculties of mind, reason, will, imagination, and feeling, it is the author's belief that we are joined to all that is. The practice of contemplative love within our own inner life brings all the levels of relationship in which we are involved into our minds and holds them before the love of God. For this reason, the author speaks of the practice of contemplative love also nurturing practical goodness. What are the problem areas that will surface in our inner prayer as we seek to stand naked before the love of God? They are issues of relationship. Interior relationship issues will surface as the unfinished guilts and unresolved longings of past and present relationships. Interior issues will surface as the psychological habits and complexes of sadness, of rage, of fear, of hurt that we have accumulated since infancy. Exterior issues will surface in our inner prayer, particularly the questions of vocation: where in the world is God calling us to invest our active service of reconciling love? All of that will come to mind as we practice contemplative love in our inner and outward life. To all those questions and issues, we will answer our one word of love. For all those arenas we invite divine insight, light, love, and blessing.

The Cloud of Unknowing closes with this word of clarification about the aim of our spiritual life. The author quotes from St. Augustine: "the entire life of a good Christian is nothing less than holy desire" (146). The practice of Centering Prayer leads us in the way of acknowledging the source of all desire, the desire for God, the desire for divine love to pierce our veil of unknowing, the desire to be clear about our direction of service. Holy desire is the heart of the practice of Centering Prayer, the desire for God's *shalom* to all of creation.

Such an undertaking is at the heart of our soul's longing, yet to undertake it consciously may seem overwhelming to us. The author is aware of the struggles we are likely to encounter. He suggests that we undertake the task of contemplative love, not with a heavy heart, but with playfulness. We are working chiefly with the will, turning our attention in a particular direction. The will is "your principal spiritual faculty" and it needs only a "fraction of a moment to move toward the object of its desire" (49). So our initial practice of Centering Prayer may require some concerted attention to willfully train our minds toward God. Yet we must not do so in a way that sets our minds to further quarrelling within ourselves.

> Rely more on joyful enthusiasm than on sheer brute force. For the more joyfully you work, the more humble and spiritual your contemplation becomes, whereas when you morbidly drive yourself, the fruits will be gross and unnatural. So be careful. Surely anyone who presumes to approach this lofty mountain of contemplative prayer through sheer brute force will be driven off with stones. (106-7).

The attitude suggested is instead a playful attitude. The author speaks of "the delight of the Lord's playfulness" (107). We enter into the contemplative arena to be at play with God. "For like a father frolicking with his son, [God] will hug and kiss one who comes to him with a child's heart" (ibid.). "And so diligently persevere until you feel joy in it" (48).

As we turn inward in contemplative practice we are confronted with our deepest pains and our own struggles for authentic life; the author gives us two different types of suggestions. He cites Mary Magdalene as an example for contemplatives. We should not only repent but actually be willing to allow ourselves to be forgiven and to be turned toward the joy of contemplative love.

> No matter how grievously a [person] has sinned, [we] can repent and amend [our] life. And if [we feel] God's grace drawing [us] on to a contemplative life . . ., let no one dare call [us] presumptuous for reaching out to God in the darkness of that cloud of unknowing with the humble desire of [divine] love. For did not our Lord say to Mary, who represents all repentant sinners called to contemplation: "Your sins are forgiven." Do you think he said this only because she was so mindful of her past sins; or because of the humility she felt at the sight of her misery; or because her sorrow was so great? No, it was because "she loved much." (69)

At the root of Mary's misery, as at the root of our misery, is our lost love of God. Mary's redemption comes because she becomes so absorbed in her love of the Lord that all else falls away. "So absorbed did she become in love that often she forgot whether she had been sinner or innocent" (70). Such absorption in contemplative love heals the roots of our sin. There are times, however, in our practice of contemplative prayer, as well as in the day-to-day rounds of our life, when the healing balm of contemplative love is truly absent. There will be times when we cannot find even a gentle stirring of love within us. The author does not ask us in those times to deny our experience. Instead, we are asked to turn our attention to sin itself as the contemplative focus. We learn in these times "experiential humility" (89). That challenging meditation can come upon us as frustration with the Centering Prayer practice or it can come as a direct experience of the sadness of life. There will be times when nothing we can do will be able to turn our quarrelling thoughts toward God in love. The author suggests, for these times:

When you feel utterly exhausted from fighting your thoughts, say to yourself: "It is futile to contend with them any longer," and then fall down before them like a captive or coward. For in doing this you commend yourself to God in the midst of your enemies and admit the radical impotence of your nature. I advise you to remember this device particularly, for in employing it you make yourself completely supple in God's hands. (88-89)

Finally, at the depths of sin, that root that must be met and overcome by divine love, is the sorrow that we do not dwell eternally within God's love, that our minds are separated from that continual blessing. Indeed, only when we have on occasion been touched by that divine light of God and have tasted of this ineffable experience, do we begin to know the root of our suffering. For these times, meditation on the word "sin" is as useful as meditating on the word "God."

Every [person] has plenty of cause for sorrow but [that one] alone understands the deep universal reason for sorrow who experiences *that [one] is*. Every other motive pales beside this one. [That person] alone feels authentic sorrow who realizes not only *what [one] is but that [one] is* . . . . In a word, [that person] feels the burden of [oneself] so tragically that he [or she] no longer cares about [oneself] if only he [or she] can love God.... Everyone must sooner or later realize in some manner both this sorrow and this longing to be freed. (103-4)

I understand the author to take us here into the essence of human suffering. The *fact* that we are creatures means that there is a distance between ourselves and God. The rift within our hearts is a *fact* of human existence. The sorrow we feel over being so filled with our own self-absorption that there is little room for the joy of divine love is the essential starting point for our healing. This rift is the root of sin. It can only be overcome through allowing it to be present and weeping through it.

We do not face this existential sorrow, however, bereft of hope. This feeling of sorrow is not the same as a desire to take one's life or a desire not to be a human being. The author states this struggle in the following words:

And yet in all this, never does [one] desire not to
be, for this is the devil's madness and blasphemy
against God. In fact, [this person] rejoices that he
[or she] is and from the fullness of a grateful heart
. . . gives thanks to God for the gift and the goodness of . . . existence. At the same time, however,
[such a person] desires unceasingly to be freed
from the knowing and feeling of [one's] being....
[God] will instruct [him or her] little by little until
[this one is] completely one in the fullness of his
love — that fullness possible on earth with [divine]
grace. (104)

RECEIVING OUR OWN CONTEMPLATIVE WORK

Each of us will respond to the work of contemplative love
in our own ways. For some this practice will be most natural; for some it is most difficult. St. Teresa of Avila spoke of
some individuals to whom the contemplative work is so
natural that once exposed to it they seem to exceed others
who have been struggling with prayer for years.

The Cloud of Unknowing speaks of two types of
contemplatives. One is like Moses, who must labor up the
mountain into the cloud of revelation. There he awaits God,
receives revelation, struggles down the mountain, smashes
the tablets of his revelation because he sees his people
falsely worshiping. Then once again Moses struggles up the
mountain. Moses is contrasted with his brother Aaron,
whose task as priest is simply to dwell in the holy of holies
with the Ark of the Covenant.

Before he was permitted to gaze upon the Ark and
to receive its design, Moses had to climb the long,
weary path up the mountain and abide there at
work in a dark cloud for six days. On the seventh
day, the Lord gave him the design for the Ark's con-
struction. In this long toil Moses endured and in
the much delayed enlightenment he finally received, we may see the pattern of those who seem
to labor so long before reaching the heights of contemplation and to relish it in its fullness but seldom.
Yet what Moses gained with such great cost and
enjoyed so rarely was Aaron's with seemingly little
toil. For his office as priest allowed him to enter
the Holy of Holies and to gaze on the Ark as often
as he liked. Aaron then represents the folk men-

tioned earlier who by their spiritual wisdom and the assistance of divine grace enjoy the perfect fruit of contemplation as often as they like. (141)

Each of us is invited into the contemplative work of love. It may evoke great struggle. We may unearth depths of pain that call for deep healing. We may find areas of pain in our relationships, requiring a lengthy process of forgiveness. We may find moments of sheer delight in the blessing of God. We may find a heart ready to flame into love. This work will come to us individually, as we are graced to receive it.

While the work on our own personality and the work of healing personal relationships may not be so demanding for some, the work of contemplative love required of us may be at the collective levels of suffering. My experience with Centering Prayer is that it can be one of the most profound ways of offering our prayers of intercession. When we are asked to bless with love whatever comes to mind, we may find that the sufferings of others will fill our minds from time to time. We may use the same form of blessing that we would with any other form of pain that comes to mind. We surround it with love and divine blessing until it is ready to be released into the cloud of forgetting. I believe that God will not leave unattended a heart full of love and offered in the service of reconciling love. In fact, I think we may expect that our early experience with Centering Prayer may focus on our own needs for personal healing. Then, after we have received a certain degree of peace within ourselves, we will be given the invitation by God to offer our hearts for the work of contemplative love on behalf of the suffering of others. The work of Centering Prayer is truly the work of the Holy Spirit, guiding our minds and hearts into those arenas in need of blessing and healing. As intermediate beings, we offer our hearts as the crucible for the healing of the world.

A final word is in order about the nature of "letting go." The practice of Centering Prayer focuses on the notion of blessing whatever comes to mind and then letting it go into the cloud of forgetting. There is a very delicate balance in this work between letting go in order to penetrate more deeply into the essence of God and letting go in order to avoid dealing with some painful or difficult image. I recall our discussion in Chapter Three on concentration and mindfulness forms of meditation. Centering Prayer, when practiced in a balanced way, is an extraordinary blend of concentration and mindfulness. We repress nothing with Centering Prayer. We allow all things to surface. We bless all things with contemplative love. Yet we simultaneously look for God within and beyond all things and all thoughts. What I suggest about the principle of 'letting go' is that we really surrender our own wills in this practice to God. There are certain troubling things, similar to Paul's thorn in the flesh, that will not go away easily. We may forever be making a modest peace with them, yet not really be able to be fully healed of them. There may be issues with which we struggle for years or days or months. Finally they are blessed and pass away from our minds. We may find these dynamics at work when we practice Centering Prayer. There may be some issues that pass rather easily through our minds, receive the loving blessing, and release into the cloud of forgetting. There may be other issues over which we will need earnestly to pray and struggle, for which the blessing of love may seem impossible. Our task is simply to offer ourselves humbly to God in prayer for our hearts and minds to be utilized as needed for the spread of contemplative love. Whether we are graced with moments of deep silent light or our prayer is filled with the struggle to bring reconciling love into a seemingly impossible situation is finally not important. What is important is that again and again we offer ourselves, heart, mind, soul, and body, to God as intermediate being, to be a channel of divine blessing.

> Whoever wishes to follow Christ perfectly must also be willing to expend [oneself] in the spiritual work of love for the salvation of all brothers and sisters in the human family. I repeat, not only for [our] friends and family and those most dear to [us], but with universal affection [we] must work for the salvation of all [humankind]. For Christ died to save anyone who repents of sin and seeks the mercy of God. So you see, contemplative love is so refined and integral that it includes in itself perfectly both humility and charity. For the same reasons and in the same way, it perfectly includes every other virtue as well. (82)

May God grace us with the call to engage in the work of contemplative love, and may we be led to service through this powerful means of prayer.

CHAPTER EIGHT

Dynamics of Inner Healing

CENTERED IN ETERNITY

As we bring our discussion of Christian meditation and inner healing to a close, I will seek to bring forward the most essential aspects of Christian meditation practice, as well as setting forth some practical guidelines for inner healing work.

The single most important aspect of Christian meditation is the cultivation of an attitude that keeps our lives centered in eternity. The practitioners of meditative prayer in Christian tradition have spoken of cultivating the attitude of constant prayer. Based on St. Paul's admonition that we should "pray without ceasing," the early desert monastics, as well as practitioners through the centuries, have suggested that what we are finally aiming toward in our prayer life is a sense of the constant presence of God. The fruit of Christian meditation practice is to be fully alive to the world, while also centered in eternity - centered in God - moment to moment, day to day, in the market, at home, at the workplace. When we remember, moment to moment, to call ourselves into the eternal reality, our lives can be filled with divine presence and the pressures of false deadlines and unnecessary conflicts can dissolve. A prayer phrase that we use for meditation in the privacy of our prayer time can become a reminder during a hectic day of the broader calling of God to us; it helps to put our moment-to-moment tasks into the context of the realities of divine service. The cultivation of *hesychasm* is thus brought into the mundane.

As we speak of inner healing through Christian meditation practice, this central theme of remembering that our lives are not lived for ourselves alone, but under the calling of eternity, becomes itself a healing balm. Nature is

104

enormously helpful in this respect. For this reason, the practice of meditating on God in creation is critical. We are renewed, our priorities restored, and our bodies and spirits lifted as we spend time in nature. At the ocean, in the mountains, in the prairies, in communion with the trees and with animals, we are brought back to the realization that human life is only one form of life and that our very pressing human concerns must be held in the context of the broader life of the world and of the universe. We have a tendency to immerse ourselves in our tasks and problems and become very myopic in these concerns. A few days or even a few hours in nature can restore our equilibrium, particularly as we see beyond the forms of nature to the "footprints" of God that nature reveals.

Christian meditation in all its forms reminds us that our lives are not our own, but are lived under the call of a divine source and power that is seeking to renew individual and social life, to give birth afresh, in every generation and in every moment, to life abundant. Whenever we call ourselves into this divine presence, we submit ourselves afresh to creative service and to transformation of ourselves. Therein also lies enormous potential for inner healing. Often as we take ourselves into the crucible of meditative awareness, we discover that the problem with which we began our search for God was not the problem that was at the bottom of our struggle. A new theme, perhaps from a different point of view or a deeper manifestation of the problem, begins to surface. Then we begin to find a solution. Each act of meditative awareness is an act of surrender to God to use our hearts and minds and bodies during that time as is needed for the healing of the world. We may find ourselves deeply involved in intercession or in problem solving or in wrestling with an old and recurring personal wound or any other agenda that seems to present itself. Our task is to receive all of that in the attitude of contemplative love and to let God work through our own awareness in bringing solutions.

Solutions may come to mind while we are about our daily tasks as well as while we are in prayer. Such a blending of prayer and action is to be hoped for. While we are busily engaged in the tasks of the day may be the time when the sudden solution of the problem emerges. While we are engaged in physical activity, whether related to our work or to an exercise regime, is a time when such insights seem to occur with regularity.

Our dream life also becomes a source of inspiration and creativity when approached with an attitude of reverence and respect. Dreams abound in Scripture as vehicles for God to speak to us. Our dreams have a language form of their own. One of our first tasks in befriending our dreams is to seek to understand our own dream symbolism. What does our dream language seem to convey? We will find a good deal of similarity between the type of imagery that sometimes occurs in deep meditation and our own dream life. As mentioned in our chapter on the nature of human consciousness, "Recovering the Soul," the realm of inner imagination is activated in imaginational forms of meditation on Scripture. The images awakened there can bear a strong similarity to our own dream images. Working with our dreams brings our imagination alive and enables us to listen more clearly to the inner messages of the soul.

We thus bring to all the aspects of our lives an attitude of surrender to God. We seek the guidance that is available in sleeping and in waking, in activity and in quiet, in conversation with others and in solitude. We listen always and everywhere for the Word of God. Life itself becomes prayer.

ESTABLISHING A REGULAR SPIRITUAL PRACTICE

For many of us there will be a time in our lives when intensive spiritual practice seems to call to us. It will be a time in which it seems especially important to devote much of our energy and our time to inner-life development. Such a time may last for a few years. During this time, we may find ourselves immersed in our inner healing work, recovering and healing the psychological wounds of childhood, dealing with chronic physical symptoms or life-threatening illness, or dealing with the frustration of broken relationships or the collapse or success of business. Perhaps we simply feel an emptiness within and want to discover the fullness of the inner Christian life for ourselves. Perhaps we have had an awakening to the inner Christ and are eager to learn more. In those times we may be very ready to undertake a daily time of meditative prayer. We are ready to enter into Mansions III of St. Teresa's *Interior Castle*, where we begin to take responsibility for our spiritual growth and lessen our dependence on external factors. The following suggestions give some guidelines for developing a regular time of meditative prayer, while also setting the stage for integrating this formal time of prayer with our daily lives.

1. It is very helpful to find one place that is your regular place for meditative prayer. It is like making a sanctuary for yourself. Create a "sacred space" for yourself through

the use of pictures, symbols, candles, etc. Some ritual of beginning, such as lighting a candle, touches our senses and reminds our whole being that we are entering into worship.

2. Do not rush away right after your prayer time. If possible, have a time following your formal prayer in which you can continue your meditation while moving about and doing simple tasks. This practice begins to bridge the inner and outer worlds, enabling us to enter more easily into "constant prayer" while about all our duties in the world.

3. Set aside twenty to thirty minutes for daily meditation. During that time, you may engage in one of the meditative prayer forms described in this book: meditation on God in creation, meditation on Scripture, the Jesus Prayer or Prayer on the Holy Name, or Centering Prayer. These prayer forms all emphasize our receptivity to God, coming to God without agenda. You will need to find your own way of integrating more active forms of prayer, such as intercession, into this practice. Some people have found it helpful to begin their prayer time with their intercessory concerns and then to move toward a more receptive form of meditation. Others have found it best to begin with the receptive form and then allow the intercessory concerns to emerge from the inner silence. Still others find themselves alternating within their prayer time between a receptive prayer practice and making their active prayers.

In general it will be useful to settle on one particular form of meditative prayer and to use it for some time to cultivate consistency. In a book like this you are exposed to a number of forms of meditative prayer. You will probably wish to experiment with each of them. After such an exposure, it will be helpful to pick one form and to stay with it for at least one month to let it begin to influence your awareness.

4. Integrate some form of physical exercise with your meditative prayer time. This might be as simple as a few stretching exercises, side bends, and toe touches. It might be a brief hatha yoga routine. It might be integrating your meditation with an existing jogging or walking practice. Quiet meditation tends to help us explore our thoughts and feelings in a deep way. Movement helps us integrate that new insight into our active lives.

5. Keep a "meditation journal." This is the single most helpful thing you can do when beginning a daily discipline. Simply note the time of day of your meditation, the form of meditation with which you worked, and a brief description of what happened. Initially, you will probably notice a great

deal of "mental clutter." Our minds typically operate at a very fast pace. Ideas race here and there. After a while, the mind slows, we get to more feelings and depth in ourselves. The meditation journal will give you a record of the changes happening within yourself. There can be significant change in only a few weeks. Even though the change may seem very slow to you, you can look back in the journal and compare what is now happening with your previous experience.

6. Bring your whole self — body, mind, feelings — into the meditation. If the meditation seems dry or too mental, ask yourself what you are feeling emotionally or physically at the time.

7. Don't try to do all this at once! Be gentle with yourself, and let your own ritual of daily prayer unfold.

KEEPING A JOURNAL

In the directives for establishing a daily prayer practice, the suggestion is given to keep a meditation journal. This device is particularly useful in the early stages of meditation practice. When you are seeking to establish some discipline and routine, it is very helpful and reinforcing to be able to look back after a few weeks and then a few months to see that your awareness has actually changed. In the early stages of a meditation journal, you will probably have many fairly discouraging entries such as, "never really got into it," "mind very busy," "wondered when the time would be up." After a few weeks, however, you will find many more entries such as, "struggled to forgive. . .," "felt calm and centered," "surrounded by Christ's love," "became aware of painful childhood memory," "prayed for peace," and so forth. As suggested by my examples, the meditation journal can have very brief entries and still be significant.

You can, of course, use a journal very effectively in a much more involved way to assist you in sorting through themes and issues.

Some of the possibilities are mentioned below.

Journal work with Scripture. An intriguing alternative to *lectio divina* meditation is to enter into the same spirit but with a pen and paper nearby. As you come upon the text or phrase of Scripture that attracts your attention, begin to write. Let the journal writing come free-form. You will begin to notice thoughts and associations that will emerge that will surprise you. If you feel there is some point at which your writing stops being meaningful, you can pause, return to the Scripture, meditate, and resume writing.

108

Journal work during meditation. Some people find it distracting to write during meditation, others find it extremely helpful to have paper and pen handy. During the meditation, a thought or insight or creative idea may come that you would like to remember. Rather than straining to remember it, write it down, and then return to the meditation.

Journal work following meditation. A meaningful adjunct to meditation is to write afterward. This writing can begin with the meditation log, but proceed with more associations on the content of the meditation. You may find that shifting the mode from meditation to writing enables you to make new discoveries on the themes on which you are working. Another important tool in journal work is drawing. Often if you will begin to draw an image that comes in meditation, it will begin to unfold and create a new revelation.

Journal work with dreams and dream images. Dream journals provide an ongoing synopsis of our inner pilgrimage. One can begin a dream journal by issuing an invitation to the unconscious to give dreams. Simply buying a special journal and keeping it beside your bed may be enough. Some people find it helpful in beginning to recall dreams to use a tape recorder. In the middle of the night, they can catch a dream fragment or dream and talk into the recorder. To start catching dreams upon awakening, it is helpful to have a bit of leisure at waking. You have dreamed each dream with your body in a particular posture. Experiment with turning to one side and then another, on your back and stomach, spending some time in each posture. Finally, if you remember only one thing, like a feeling or a single word or theme, write it down. That says to your dream life that you are interested and want to cultivate a relationship.

There is a useful formula for working with dreams and with dream images that is simple yet significant. This formula can be applied equally to a meditation image as to a dream. You may be a person who has images appear in meditation. Sometimes you will immediately know what these images mean. At other times, you may feel that it is important to try to understand the image. You can take your work with the image forward through this process.

Step 1. Treat the dream or meditation image objectively. What is its own inherent message? If you look at the dream as a whole, what is it trying to say? Try to capture as much detail as possible. Often the "aha" of meaning for the dream is received when you notice a particular placement of something or someone in the dream. Notice the details of buildings and settings. Notice clothing or nudity. Notice the relationship among objects and beings. If you were to tell the inner story of the dream, what would its theme be? In the objective analysis, you seek to bring forward as much of the inner integrity of the dream or meditation image as you can.

Step 2. What is the dream's subjective meaning? After you have explored the dream on its own terms, then ask yourself: if the dream represents me or parts of me, then what does it mean? In the subjective stage of interpretation, you take each image as related to yourself or a revelation of a portion of yourself and you ask, if I am, for example, the tree in the dream, what does that say about my present life-circumstances? In this stage, it is very helpful to draw pictures and to put yourself into postures that resemble the objects and figures in the dream. You can also engage in active dialogues between the various figures in the dreams, and also carry the dream forward into dialogue with your conscious associations with the dream images.

Step 3. Only after the first two steps do you approach the symbolic interpretation of the dream. At this stage you look for universals. In this case it can be useful to have a dictionary of dream symbolism or of mythic images. You look to see what these dream images have in common with various interpretations from mythology and from fairy tales. You look to universal themes that the dream may be presenting. There is no simple way to build our lexicon of such meanings. Reading widely in Scripture and mythology, in Jungian literature and Campbell's mythic material assists us. And it is very important to note that we can make significant progress in understanding our dreams without this stage being invoked.

Finally, a very useful tool in understanding our dreams is to begin building our personal dictionary of dream images. In this dictionary we begin by writing down recurring images and themes. After noticing them for some time, we can also begin to note the ordinary meaning of such images for us.

WORKING ALONE/SEEKING COMPANIONSHIP

The numerous suggestions given here for the meditative life are intended to facilitate individual deepening of spiritual awareness. Often circumstances dictate that we undertake our spiritual disciplines primarily as a solitary practice. I have been surprised, in the numerous retreats that I have guided, to discover the large numbers of people in our churches who have been practicing some form of meditation or meditative prayer, usually in isolation from other individuals. Often, even in the same church, people will not realize who might be a companion on this inner pilgrimage.

There are some major problems with working alone in this journey. Foremost is a sense of isolation. This isolation can also lead to an inflated sense of uniqueness, when the inner domains begin to open. We can think that we are somehow more worthy than others, not realizing that these inner experiences are normal parts of a soul's journey into God, available in different forms to everyone. We may also encounter confusing or frightening material in our inner world. Or we may be very confused when our inner life is opening and simultaneously our outer life is disintegrating. We will want to look for some companionship when possible. I have listed some of the possible ways of seeking companionship. Some will be more appealing than others; and we may find ourselves seeking different types of companionship at different times of our life.

Occasional spiritual direction. One of the ways we can gain companionship is through retreats and guided experiences with others. Even if these are short-term experiences, they can provide valuable information and we can often ask questions about our inner life that are puzzling. Through such a practice, we retain a certain autonomy within ourselves. The Holy Spirit is our primary source of guidance, yet we avail ourselves from time to time of the insight of others. My hunch is that this is actually the primary mode of spiritual guidance in our time. Its problems are that we may not be astute to our own blind spots. We may struggle needlessly on issues or problems that might be clarified with the input of worthy guides. Retreats International, (P.O. Box 1067, Notre Dame, IN 46556) publishes an excellent listing of 350 retreat centers around the country, with a lisiting of the types of retreat experiences and facilities they offer.

Ongoing spiritual direction or companionship. There are a number of individuals now equipped to provide knowledgeable spiritual guidance. Many clergy are equipped to give guidance in meditative prayer life. Many Roman Catholic monasteries provide retreat opportunities and have knowledgeable people available for spiritual guidance. Many pastoral counselors and pastoral counseling centers have the capacity to provide spiritual guidance or are able to supply referrals. Or you may begin to ask clergy in your area who seem sensitive to spiritual issues about potential sources of referral. Spiritual Directors International, (1329 Seventh Ave., San Francisco, CA 94122) publishes a national listing of members, many of whom offer spiritual direction.

Another source of guidance is a spiritual friendship, in which we obtain assistance from a companion, a peer relationship. This peer will necessarily have insights that we do not have, because of the variation in life-experience that we each bring to a relationship. As we share our inner life and our questions with one another, we can also look for assistance in understanding the places and circumstances in which we seem to be stuck.

Seeking psychotherapy or pastoral counseling. We may find ourselves severely distressed by a growing immersion in inner material, particularly as related to unresolved issues of childhood patterns of emotional, physical, or sexual abuse, or the recognition of long-term patterns of relationship problems. It may be very important to find assistance through psychotherapy or pastoral counseling to assist during these times. Pastors will be able to make local referrals. Growing attention is being given to issues of spiritual development in the field of psychotherapy and psychiatry. There are growing numbers of therapists and counselors who are equipped to journey with you into your places of inner vulnerability and who are sensitive to issues of spiritual development. The Association for Transpersonal Psychology publishes a national list of professional members, giving their areas of expertise and interest. For information, contact ATP, P. O. Box 3049, Stanford CA 94309. There is also a growing interest in the theme of spiritual emergence and spiritual emergency in the transpersonal field. The terms originated in the work of Christina and Stanislav Grof. Many individuals may find some of the spontaneous phenomena associated with spiritual emergence taking place. An excellent resource from the Grofs on this process is their book *The Stormy Search for the Self.*

Training programs in spiritual development. We are witnessing an amazing proliferation of short- and long-term training programs in spiritual development. With a bit of inquiry, you may find courses or sequences of study at area seminaries of many different denominations. San Francisco Theological Seminary provides an extensive program. It was significantly influenced by Morton Kelsey in its formative years. There are also public programs originating from monastic communities. Mercy Center in Burlingame, California, and Mt. Carmel in Dallas, Texas, provide excellent programs. There are retreat houses in many locations. Some denominations are undertaking extensive programs at the national level, such as the United Methodist Academy for Spiritual Formation (1908 Grand Ave., Nashville, TN 37202).

The Institute in Culture and Creation Centered Spirituality in Oakland, California, is directed by Matthew Fox. It provides programs of study of various lengths, with the opportunity to complete a master's degree. The Shalem Institute in Washington, D.C., was created by Tilden Edwards and Gerald May for exploring the interface between pastoral counseling, psychotherapy, and spiritual direction. It provides an extensive training in an external format. The Institute of Transpersonal Psychology in Palo Alto, California, explores the interface of psychology, spirituality, and body/mind relationship. It offers residential M.A. and Ph.D. degrees and one-year external Certificates of Spiritual Studies or Transpersonal Studies, as well as external master's degrees. At Oakwood Spiritual Life Center in Syracuse, Indiana, I offer training in Spiritual Formation and Spiritual Direction that is linked to degree programs at Garrett-Evangelical Theological Seminary in Evanston, Illinois, and with United Theological Seminary in Dayton, Ohio, as well as brief retreat experiences and spiritual direction. Our address is 702 E. Lake View Rd., Syracuse, IN 46567, phone: 219-457-5600.

WORKING WITH A GROUP

It can be a wonderful experience to join with others in cultivating a group for spiritual nurture. Such a group can be motivated by one individual. It can be guided by a trained leader or it can be a "prayer and share" group, without trained leadership. In either case, there are some guidelines that I think are important in creating a climate in which individuals are truly nourished.

1. We are meeting together to be individually nourished by God. The authority for what happens with an individual rests within herself or himself. By this I mean that there are no special requirements for disclosing any particular information to the group. Each individual is free to share as much or as little of her or his inner experience as seems appropriate at any meeting.

2. Issues of confidentiality of the group must be discussed. The group must decide how much or how little the group members are free to share about the group outside itself. There must be agreement to a plan by everyone. This commitment can be reviewed periodically. One suggestion that keeps the material confidential, yet allows for discussion about the group to significant individuals outside the group would be: individuals can talk about the kind of for-

mat the group uses, e.g., what it used for meditation, and individuals can share their own experience with others, but they cannot divulge the content of other people's experience. At two extremes are the contracts that nothing is to be shared about the group or that anything can be shared. The problem with the latter contract is that it can lead to gossip, with inevitable distortion of other people's experiences. The problem with absolute secrecy is that it can disrupt significant sharing with a spouse or spiritual friend who is not in the group.

If such a group is in a church, it seems to me to be important that it open itself periodically for new members. This keeps exclusionary problems to a minimum, and it helps to spread the meditative riches of the group into the ongoing life of the church.

3. A regular format for the group might be something like the following: (a) gathering and greeting each other, sharing from the past week, (b) a guided meditation by one of the group members or from a resource that is being used by the group, (c) time for silence with the meditation and for journal writing following the meditation, (d) sharing of experience as seems appropriate to each individual, (e) giving support, feedback, insights to each other, (f) closure for the week, attending to each other in ways that support and nourish each individual's journey (may be a short ritual, a hymn, or a prayer by an individual or open prayer within the group).

One of the most important aspects of such a group is that the sharing come out of the meditation experience. I have been truly amazed at the depth and ease of intimacy created in a group when the sharing comes from meditation experience. It is critical that each individual experience be honored for itself. There can be no hasty judgment spoken against such experience. We are in the realm of the guidance of the Holy Spirit in such a gathering. After the group becomes familiar with each other, there may well be times when you need to challenge each other, as each searches for authentic life with God, but this challenge will come best after you have shared deeply with each other over a period of time.

INNER HEALING IN MIDLIFE

We have been exploring some of the practical aspects of spiritual practice as a way of bringing our work in Christian meditation and inner healing to a conclusion. Now we bring together some of the themes and issues that we may

114

address in our inner healing work. To do so, let us return to Dante and his loss of way in midlife. Most of us drawn to this deepening spiritual life through Christian meditation have come through the gateway of inner-life awakening at midlife. Dante sheds much light on this passage.

"Mid-way this way of life we're bound upon, I woke to find myself in a dark wood, Where the right road was wholly lost and gone" (*L'Inferno*, I:1-3, 1949, 71). Dante wrote these lines opening the *Divine Comedy* during his own midlife crisis. At the age of thirty-five he was banished from his native Florence because of political conflicts. His interior journey took him into the realm of an underworld, where he confronted the demonic evil of life, into a realm of moral purification called purgatory, and into the realm of paradise where he met the divine in the form of saints, the apostles, Christ, and ultimately in a full union with primal love. His visionary guide in paradise was Beatrice, a woman whom he had met in life, who served as intermediary for Dante while he grew accustomed to the radiant splendor of the heavenly realm.

Dante's midlife crisis has given us a rich tapestry of the soul. We are the richer because he lost his way, because the chosen path he thought he was going to trod was blocked, and he was forced to undergo the full entry into a world beyond time, the inner world of the demonic and angelic realms.

Dante's understanding of the stages of life (Campbell 1968b, 633-34) is illuminating to our successful passage through these midlife challenges. The first stage of life he called Youth, in which we are taught the basic perspectives of our society and equipped to lead our adult lives. His second stage I will call Adulthood. Adulthood takes place roughly between the ages of twenty-five and forty-five. In adulthood, one passes through midlife simultaneously doing service to society and to one's family and undergoing a spiritual awakening. Adulthood prepares us for Age, beginning roughly at age forty-five and extending to age seventy. In the period of Age, we make our most valuable contributions to our culture — awakened spiritually and skilled in the necessary political and social capacities to be agents of change. The period of Age is dramatically increasing for many in our time into their eighties and nineties. Retirement offers for many a marvelous opportunity to review and reorient one's life of active service in the world, while perhaps also making more time for contemplative life. By living Age well we are enabled to move into Decrepitude, when it comes, feeling that we have made the contributions that were ours to make and freely turning our attention to the full contemplation of the divine, as we begin our journey toward death.

The passage from a known way of relating to reality to the realms beyond the ordinary has been given many names. Historically, it has been occasioned by conversions, a sudden awareness of the potential for direct access to the Holy. It has been given the name "awakening" by many traditions. Evelyn Underhill, in her work *Mysticism*, characterizes it as the Awakening of the Self. The disjuncture between known adult realities and the possibilities of the other world of interior development has been recently called spiritual emergence. It has found its most popular context in Western culture as one of many possible shifts of consciousness accompanying the midlife crisis. For Jung, it was the discovery that what we had once assumed was the totality of our consciousness was in essence only our persona. Once discovered, the unconscious Self calls to us to be explored.

Dante's characterization of this midlife change as a losing of one's way is equally applicable, whether we speak of an external losing of one's way or an internal losing of one's way. The external disjunctures in marriages, careers, the completion of tasks such as parenting, or the sudden shifts in self-awareness as we assume the responsibilities of caretaking for our aging parents or through their deaths all present the imminent danger of causing us to lose our way through the accustomed life we had set for ourselves. Internally, we may lose our way when our dream-life suddenly awakens, with images of threat or destruction or shadowy figures that terrorize our accustomed way of relating to ourselves. Or we may lose our way through an experience of divine essence so profound and so vivid that a life of hoped-for epiphany becomes realized and faith must move from the arena of belief to knowing.

Whether the disjunctures come first from the outside or from the inside, from threat or completion, we face a time of radical dislocation and the opportunity to discover the fullness of the Self. Such a time of midlife journey began for me at about the age of thirty-three. Before that time, my dream life was dormant. I was filled with good intention, spiritual and intellectual curiosity, and yet struggled even to define prayer. Schooled in the intellectual climate of the seminary during the "demythologizing" era of Scripture studies, there was room only for a bit of mystery around the spiritual life. Most interest was directed toward training us seminarians as intellectually respectable theologians and preparing us for social action. In ten years of parish ministry, weekly devoting myself to scriptural study for sermon preparation, I was prepared, as the author of *The Cloud of Unknowing* would have put it, for the deeper awareness of God, having long pondered the questions of faith.

What initially awakened for me, however, was not the deeper awareness of God; it was my own shadow self. In dreams of terror, in the painful struggle to come to terms with my disowned body and many confounding issues of sexuality, I turned wholeheartedly toward the inner life for new discoveries. I had no map for what I was experiencing, so I turned to Jung in his work with dreams, I turned to June Singer's *Androgyny*, and I learned massage and meditation. In the most painful period, I spoke of the "death of God." All the activities that had once filled me with excitement in parish ministry were now becoming repetitive. I had also filled my time with many meaningful projects of social action. Much to my amazement, when clarity came concerning my next step, it was astonishingly easy to lay aside these tasks. I was ready to jump headlong into Dante's inferno of underworld, middle-world, and upper-world inner awareness. I spoke of being like a vessel that had been well filled in my early life for the service rendered in early adulthood, but the vessel was now empty. I desperately thirsted for the discovery of the divine as a wellspring within me, offering daily resources for inspiration and sustenance. My own spiritual reserves could no longer sustain me through the deaths of parishioners who were my friends. The grief was beyond my own reserves of grace. Like Dante, I had lost my way. And, like Dante, I left all my known world behind me, moving across country to make new discoveries.

I began discovering the lost world of the Christian methods of meditative prayer that I have now been able to share through this book, together with meditation practices of many other spiritual traditions. I found the therapies of bioenergetics, bodywork, and group process. I found the doors open to inner experiences of mythic figures. At a Tibetan Buddhists' retreat, Christ as a living inner vision came alive. I found a community for my exploration of soul and body with the Institute of Transpersonal Psychology.

FIVE GATEWAYS FOR SPIRITUAL AWAKENING

I suggest that my experience is by no means isolated. Similar types of openings to inner-life realities are abounding in our time. I will briefly recapitulate the types of experience we may encounter in our inner journeys, as related to the transpersonal model of consciousness developed in Chapter Two. From this model we will see five major gateways for exploration that are possible.

This model of consciousness (Wilber 1980) speaks of a progressive development, ranging from infancy and early childhood through the capacity for adult rationality. The model does not stop there, however. It then speaks of a renewed relationship with the body in adult life, leading to a sense of body-mind integration. Inner-life awareness, beginning with a renewed capacity for imagination, leads toward subtle and causal realm experience. These are inner capacities especially related to what we have traditionally called spiritual experience. In the subtle realm, one relates to the divine in form: for example, to Christ or the holy Mother or other divine figure. This is the realm of *kataphatic* prayer, or prayer with images. Causal realm experience is the realm of *apophatic* (non-image) experience: the divine beyond form, the divine as radiant light or as the void, or as Buddha mind. The capacity for imagination, the world of dreams and creative visualization, lies between the rational mind and these inner realms of subtle and causal experience. Within this realm of imagination is the capacity for visiting our inner childhood experience and bringing forth a healing of memories. We can expect in such an awakening to inner awareness that there will be a period of major shifts and changes in the body, as traumatic memory is released and as the energy of divine presence opens our channels of awareness. We see in St. Teresa of Avila's intense body experiences, especially in her fifth and sixth mansions in the *Interior Castle*, this type of energy phenomenon in the body. I have given substantial attention to this issue in my book, *Embracing God: Praying with Teresa of Avila* (1996).

I do not mean to imply that our awakening to these levels of awareness arrives in an orderly way. No, the midlife awakening is more like an explosion of a particular perspective that can give birth to an awakened capacity for the full spectrum of the soul and for a profound relationship to the world.

Based on this model, we may speak of five distinct gateways of spiritual development that may be navigated in this midlife explosion of the soul. These gateways are the body, the personal unconscious, subtle realm experience, causal realm experience, and what I will name the "call of the ordinary."

First, we may speak of the gateway of the body. A major confrontation for many of us in midlife will be through illness and other forms of physical limitation. We see a virtual epidemic of lifestyle and stress-related illnesses in our culture: cancer, heart disease, Epstein-Barr and other types of chronic fatigue syndrome, as well as issues of infertility or childbirth. The many avenues for working with various addictions bring these issues into focus, as well. Through the messages of the body, many women and men in midlife find themselves undergoing major questioning of life purpose and lifestyle. Whether as antidotes to illness or simply as an investment in healthy living, many individuals also turn to a new relationship with their bodies through fitness programs, diet regimes, or practices such as hatha yoga. We may find, through such practices, a new intimacy with our bodies, as well as a time in our exercise to pray and examine ourselves. A primary gateway for our culture to begin exploring the realms of the mind beyond the rational has been through the near death experiences of now hundreds of thousands of people. However our relationship with our body is engaged in midlife, it is apt to bring us into new ways of relating to the more subtle energies of emotions and spiritual awareness.

A second gateway is related to our relationship to the personal unconscious and the recovery of memory related to early childhood experience. In this respect, we may think of the unfreezing of emotional expression that may accompany the recognition of early traumatization through physical or sexual abuse. What has astounded me in this respect is the willingness of the psyche to reveal this type of material when there is an environment of support and loving acceptance. In several cases, with minimal external encouragement, I have seen this type of material revealed. When the inner child is then heard and empowered, a healing of great significance can occur. Often the inner child does not realize that she or he has survived the trauma, and to encounter the mature adult she or he has become can serve to set the individual free from a sense of frozen emotional expression. Obviously the newly emerging individual will have much learning to do in order to live productively with a new level of direct access to emotion. When issues are addressed from an especially young age or from infancy, the individual may be thrown into enormous dislocation and into the issues we will see under the description of the causal experience. Much tenderness and nurturance are needed as well as skilled therapeutic work to navigate these uncharted areas. While I have spoken of the most traumatic cases here, all of us will have some work to do in this area, even when our families have been most nurturing. Inevitably, we have been misunderstood by adults when we were children and some scars remain.

A third kind of crisis accompanies the opening of subtle realm experience. In this case, the individual may be seized with visionary material that has a mythological character. In my own case, much of my inner-life explosion came in this form. I found my inner work in meditation and bioenergetic breathwork sessions often taking the form of dialogue between my conscious self-knowledge and figures such as Christ, Dionysus, Apollo, Shakti, Shiva, Buddha, and the Feminine in many guises. In one of the most dramatic periods of awakening, I spent many hours with various warriors of history understanding in a new way the potentials of the male psyche for physical and sexual aggression. Clearly, Dante's *Divine Comedy* describes this kind of awakening. In some cases material that seems to be of another life or a past life is also spontaneously present. Here, there is a need for understanding the stories that accompany such figures. There is also a need for a healthy distance from the material. The psyche is presenting in metaphoric form much that can enhance self-understanding. It is not necessary, in my view, to develop too much attachment to these experiences, as for example proving or disproving theories on reincarnation.

Subtle realm mythic adventures carry the collective pain and celebration of humanity. I found myself wondering if this inner experience was not a type of intercessory prayer, in which the ancient and modern warriors found some release as they were understood, if only within my own psyche. We need in this realm a sense of discernment of the inner voices and visions. We need to learn which of the inner figures are trustworthy. We need to learn how to interpret the divine guidance that comes in the form of allegory and metaphor.

A fourth type of crisis will accompany the immersion of the psyche into the causal realm. Here, without form, without words, we may find ourselves simultaneously exploring the unfathomable mysteries of God and making peace with our own preverbal experiences in the womb, in birthing, and in early infancy. Since our mind has entered the arena beyond words, we may struggle with the deepest levels of our own personal psychological experience, the primordial nonverbal wellspring of experience before our abilities to speak or to fathom the world of speech. In my opinion, this arena is the one classically described as the dark night of the soul, the arena in which we make our most dramatic encounter with the forces of death and the eternal dynamism of the creative God. Certainly, a crisis of this force may have enormous implications. It may take an individual weeks, months, or even years fully to work through this immersion in the infinite and bring its gifts back into the ordinary world. Much understanding, much support, and much attention to practicalities needs to be given to those working through this most profound level of awareness. This is the crisis leading to a full embrace of the divine and a full epiphany of God within the individual.

A fifth kind of crisis needs to be mentioned. It is a crisis associated with ordinary consciousness or with the capacities of the rational mind to relate and synthesize all our various modes of experience. It is the crisis of practical living among the challenges of our ordinary world, with its works and sufferings. It is the crisis of meaningful service. This fifth kind of midlife crisis involves both letting go of our self-image and of recreating a new and meaningful vocational presence in the world following a shift of inner worldview. In many cases, this experience may feel very much like taking off one persona, with its accompanying vocational and personal lifestyle choices, and putting on another. For this task of taking off and putting on our professional and personal identity, a healthy humor and self-esteem together with the capacity for reasoned choices is necessary. In 1986, after nineteen years of marriage, my wife, Ruth, and I became the parents of two infant boys. How will we serve the human family? How will we serve the ordinary realities of the world? For us the maxim was not: 'Before enlightenment, chop wood, carry water. After enlightenment, chop wood, carry water.' It was more like: 'After midlife exploration, change diapers, nurture children and aging parents.' Enlightenment is a long way away when you can't sleep from exhaustion and when tempers flare. Yet through these means my life of service has returned in full flower after what at first seemed to be a time-out from the world to attend to the soul's inner explosion of awareness.

For individuals who have been celibate, the life of relationship may call. For those childless, the fulfillment of parenthood may demand attention. For those completing the tasks of parenthood, dormant themes of personal creativity and delayed career aspirations will burst forth. A variety of challenges in the world of work may predominate. The fifth crisis, the crisis of ordinary reality is: how will I meaningfully serve the present age?

What I am proposing here is that the midlife challenge is a movement toward wholeness in which the unopened realms of the psyche wish to manifest. It may come in many forms, depending upon which type of crisis of consciousness is most prominent. The midlife task is to discover the skills and inner resources to continue to make major changes throughout the rest of life.

DISCERNING GOD'S WILL

St. Teresa of Avila concludes her *Interior Castle* by stating that the whole purpose of the deepening interior life is good works. It is seemingly a very simple conclusion to a master work of interior understanding. Yet her conclusion is ours as well. Finally, the purpose of Christian spiritual life is to dwell in harmony with God and neighbor, to be free to engage ourselves in meaningful service to God. Throughout the ages, the hallmark of Christian spiritual life has been this test: Does prayer lead to love? Does personal piety lead to creative and uplifting forms of human community? If it does not, then it is not of God; we have gotten off the true path.

Throughout our work in Christian meditation, we need to hold before ourselves this question: Is God calling me to this work? To this inner work, to this particular outer work? There may come times when we need especially to ask for guidance. I offer the following discernment process as a particular method, rooted in the style of Ignatian discernment. I am indebted to Nicola Kester for this particular outline (1985). I have adapted the outline into a process for discernment.

The process invites the participation of our whole spectrum of awareness, the rational, emotional, imaginal qualities of our mind, as well as physical awareness. The first principle is that we earnestly desire to seek God's will and guidance beyond our own conscious deliberations on a theme or issue.

This first principle of discernment is the cultivating of an attentive, receptive, listening attitude toward God. The more sincerely we have devoted ourselves to our meditative prayer life, the more sensitive these awarenesses will be within us. Entering into a discernment process is predicated on this active attention to divine will and the human willingness to listen and be led.

To begin this discernment process, state the problem or issue on which you wish to seek guidance in a simple way. If possible, give it a yes or no outcome or two distinct outcomes. If you cannot see your way to limit the outcomes to two, then undertake no more than three outcomes with one process. Utilize the discernment process more than once on the same theme exploring other outcomes. For example, you may be asking a question regarding continuing at a particular place of employment. Or a question exploring two or three options for employment or for particular aspects of work about which you must make a choice.

After you have stated the options, write them down. Under each option, list all the factors of which you are consciously aware that will influence your decision one way or the other for this choice. You need not be too precise in how you make your list; simply spend time with the options listing the various factors and ramifications of which you are aware. This engages our rational thought process into the discernment process. Most likely this step will come fairly readily, as you have already been thinking a good deal on the decision. However, be open for surprises as well. Often, simply by making a list side by side of these kinds of outcomes, we make some new discoveries.

After your lists seem complete, take a short break from the process. Now go back and take one set of comments on one of the outcomes. Review your comments, asking yourself how you feel as you read these comments. This aspect of the discernment process draws in the emotions. Also ask yourself for a physical or bodily or gut reaction to what you read. Write down these responses at the end of the list. Take a brief break and go to the other list or lists of other outcomes and spend time individually with each one, going through the same process of listening emotionally and physically for your reactions.

You may be noticing at this stage that you seem to be leaning in one direction or another, but do not stop the process yet. There is more to come. Now quiet yourself, enter into meditation, go gently but certainly into the arena that you have come to trust as that place within where you encounter God. Use your most natural form of meditation, Centering Prayer, the Jesus Prayer, or a favorite passage of Scripture for meditation. After a few moments of quiet, go back to the first outcome with its accompanying list and emotional/physical responses. Review only one list at a time. Review the first list in its totality and then inwardly ask yourself for a symbol or an image of this outcome. Be open to what comes. Write it down at the bottom of the list. Do not censure what comes. I have seen many surprising turns at this point. Sometimes a humorous image comes or something seemingly completely unrelated. Just make a note of it and proceed on. Center and quiet yourself again, letting go of the first outcome. Then do this process with the second list, fully devoting your attention to the list and to your previous emotional and physical reactions, and ask for a symbol or image of this outcome, receiving it and writing it down. If you have another outcome, proceed in the same way with it.

Now again center yourself in your meditation, turning yourself in prayer toward God for an answer to your dilemma. Invoke Christ's presence or the divine in another form, if that is more directly accessible to you. Present each symbol or image now, one at a time, to Christ. Look for that one that gives you and Christ more pleasure. Which is finally most pleasing to you both? Looking for that which is most pleasing to Christ is a mainstay of Ignatian discernment.

You will no doubt by this time have received many inner "ahas" as you have seen many aspects of the decision, but continue to pray and listen inwardly for clarity. Often by this time you will see that this decision only reflects a deeper issue for you, which now comes to light to be explored. Often you will find that the divine guidance suggests that this is a decision that you are genuinely free to make either way. Sometimes you will find some very surprising suggestions coming from Christ. What has surprised me over the years, in exploring this discernment process with many individuals, is that when we have earnestly cultivated our inner life, the inner Christ will give us most generally very healthy advice. Our way will be made clear.

There is a final step, which is testing our own inner guidance with another person. This step is absolutely necessary if your guidance suggests a path that will have impact on others. If your decision process will involve others in a way that would ultimately involve some decision over their lives, then you must directly consult with them. If the decision is not so directly related to impacting others, it is still advisable to discuss your process with a trusted companion. Often more discoveries will be revealed in this process, or you will find that your companion has unknown resources to assist you in this particular domain.

Finally, St. Teresa gives this directive on when to trust our inner guidance. The word of God or the inner guidance for St. Teresa is genuine when it effects what it says. In other words, there is external validation. There is no discrepancy between inner guidance and external manifestation or between inner awareness and inner certainty. Another way to put it is that you know with clarity that this is now the correct path. Our inner uncertainty, confusion, or anxiety has been relieved with the giving of the divine answer.

As we undertake our own inner healing and the healing of the world through Christian meditation practice, we will encounter many areas of confusion and many new places within ourselves for exploration and many new arenas in our world for service. We will follow the One who is the Way, the Truth, and the Life, as we turn with humility again and again for guidance along the way, the guidance of trusted companions, the guidance of Scripture, and the guidance of the inner divine presence.

We seek to be agents of the new heaven and the new earth promised in the final chapters of the Book of Revelation, actualizing these in the political realities of the world and in the individual human being. We claim the divine promise, each to be marked on our foreheads with God's presence. We are racing against time, in our age, to embrace all the realms of the interior, so that they do not subvert us into unconscious annihilation. We are seeking to embrace the divine seeking each of us, opening our hearts and minds to the fullness of our capacity to interrelate to all that is.

Our hope is that the explosion of inner-life awareness, so compellingly obvious in our time, is being ignited by God to bring us into the twenty-first century as people of compassion, hope, and joy.

May the stories we are each writing within our inner and outer lives be as enriching to the human story as was Dante's story: the story he wrote, when he was willing to be totally lost in a dark wood, until he found his way into divine love.

Bibliography

Assagioli, R.1977. *Psychosynthesis: A Manual of Principles and Techniques.* New York: Penguin.

Bettelheim, B.1977. *The Uses of Enchantment: The Meaning and Importance of Fairy Tales.* New York: Vintage.

Brownell, B. 1950. *The Human Community: Its Philosophy and Practice for a Time of Crisis.* New York: Harper & Bros.

Campbell, J.1968a. *The Hero with a Thousand Faces.* 2d ed. Princeton, N.J.: Princeton University Press.

—————. 1968b. *The Masks of God*, vol. 4, *Creative Mythology.* New York: Viking.

Capra, F. 1975. *The Tao of Physics: An Exploration of the Parallels between Modern Physics and Eastern Mysticism.* New York: Bantam.

A Course in Miracles. 1975. Huntington Station, N.Y.: Foundation for Inner Peace.

Cousins, E., trans.1978. *Bonaventure: The Soul's Journey into God, the Tree of Life, the Life of St. Francis.* New York: Paulist Press.

Dante Alighieri.1949. *The Comedyof DanteAlighieri, the Florentine, Cantica I, Hell (Il Inferno).* Trans. D. L. Sayers. New York: Penguin.

—————. 1955. *The Comedy of Dante Alighieri the Florentine, Cantica II, Purgatory (Il Purgatorio).* Trans. D. L. Sayers. New York: Penguin.

—————. 1962. *The Comedy of Dante Alighieri, the Florentine, Cantica III, Paradise (Il Paradiso).* Trans. D. L. Sayers and B. Reynolds. New York: Penguin.

DelBene, R., and H. Montgomery. 1981. *The Breath of Life.* New York: Harper & Row.

Fox, M. 1980. *Breakthrough: Meister Eckhart's Creation Spirituality in New Translation.* Garden City, N.Y.: Doubleday.

—————.1983. *Original Blessing: A Primer in Creation Spirituality.* Santa Fe: Bear & Co.

French, R. M., trans. 1952. *The Way of a Pilgrim and the Pilgrim Continues His Way.* 2d ed. Minneapolis: Seabury Press.

Goldstein, J. 1976. *The Experience of Insight: A Natural Unfolding*. Santa Cruz, Calif.: Unity.

Goleman, D.1988. *TheMeditativeMind*. Rev. ed. LosAngeles:J. P. Tarcher.

Grof, C. & S. Grof. 1992. *The Stormy Search for the Self: A Guide to Personal Growth through Transformational Crisis*. New York: Tarcher Putnam.

Guigo II. 1978. *The Ladder of Monks, a Letter on the Contemplative Life, and Twelve Meditations*. Trans. E. Colledge and J. Walsh. Garden City, N.Y.: Image Books.

Hillman, J.1975. *Re-Visioning Psychology*. New York: Harper & Row.

The Holy Bible, new revised standard version.1989. Grand Rapids, Mich.: Zondervan.

The Holy Bible, revised standard version.1946, 1952. New York: American Bible Society.

Johnston, W., ed. 1973. *The Cloud of Unknowing and the Book of Privy Counseling*. Garden City, N.Y.: Doubleday.

Judy, D. H. 1996. *Embracing God: Praying with Teresa of Avila*. Nashville, TN: Abingdon.

Jung, C. G. *The Collected Works of C. G Jung*. 2d ed. Trans. R. F. C. Hull. Bollingen Series 20. Princeton, N.J.: Princeton University Press.

————.1967. *Symbols of Transformation:An Analysis of the Prelude to a Case of Schizophrenia*. Vol. 5.

————. 1966. *Two Essays on Analytical Psychology*. Vol. 7.

————. 1969. *Four Archetypes: Mother, Rebirth, Spirit, Trickster*. Vol. 9, part I.

————. 1968. *Aion: Researches into the Phenomenology of the Self*. Vol. 9, part II.

Kadloubovsky, E., and G. E. H. Palmer, trans.1954. *Early Fathers from the Philokalia*. London and Boston: Faber.

Kavanaugh, K., and O. Rodriguez, trans. 1973. *The Collected Works of St. John of the Cross*. Washington, D.C.: ICS Publications.

————.1980. *The Collected Works of St. Teresa of Avila*. Vol.2. Washington, D.C.: ICS Publications.

Kelsey, M. T.1976. *The Other Side of Silence:AGuide to Christian Meditation*. New York: Paulist Press.

Kester, N. 1985. *"Meeting the Angel: The Annunciation as a Model of Conscious Surrender."* Menlo Park, Calif.: Institute of Transpersonal Psychology, doctoral dissertation, unpublished.

Merton, T., trans. 1960. *The Wisdom of the Desert*. New York: A New Directions Book.

CHRISTIAN MEDITATION AND INNER HEALING

Michael, C., and M. Norrisey. 1991. *Prayer and Temperament: Different Prayer Forms for Different Personality Types.* Charlottesville, Va.: The Open Door.

A Monk of New Clairvaux. 1979. *Don't You Belong To Me?* New York: Paulist Press.

Mottola, A., trans.1964. *The Spiritual Exercises of St. Ignatius.* Garden City, N.Y.: Doubleday-Image.

Needleman, J. 1980. *Lost Christianity.* Garden City, N.Y.: Doubleday.

The New English Bible. 1971. New York: Cambridge University Press.

Pennington, M. B. 1980. *Centering Prayer: Renewing an Ancient Christian Prayer Form.* Garden City, N.Y.: Doubleday.

Singer, J. 1973. *Boundaries of the Soul: The Practice of Jung's Psychology.* Garden City, N.Y.: Doubleday.

———. 1977. *Androgyny: Toward a New Theory of Sexuality.* Garden City, N.Y.: Anchor.

Sugden, E., ed. 1921, 1968. *The Standard Sermons of John Wesley.* Vol. 2. London: Epworth Press.

Underhill, E. 1999. *Mysticism: A Study in the Nature and Development of Man's Spiritual Consciousness.* Oxford, England: Penguin.

Vaughan, F. 1986. *The InwardArc: Healing and Wholeness in Psychotherapy and Spirituality.* Boston and London: Shambhala.

Walsh, R., and F. Vaughan, eds.1980. *Beyond Ego: Transpersonal Dimensions in Psychology.* Los Angeles: Tarcher.

Wakefield, G., ed.1983. *The WestminsterDictionary of Christian Spirituality* Philadelphia: WestTninster Press.

Wesley, C. 1989. "Jesus, Lover of My Soul." *The United Methodist Hymnal: Book of United Methodist Worship.* Nashville: The United Methodist Publishing House, #479.

Wilber, K. 1980. *The Atman Project: A Transpersonal View of Human Development.* Wheaton, Ill.: Theosophical Publishing House, Quest.

———. 1981a. *No Boundary: Eastern and Western Approaches to Personal Growth.* Boulder and London: Shambhala.

———. 1981b. *Up from Eden: A Transpersonal View of Human Evolution* Garden City, N.Y.: Anchor.

Additional Resources

Historic Resources and Overview

Foster, R. J. & J. B. Smith, ed. 1990. *Devotional Classics, Selected Readings for Individuals & Groups*. San Francisco: HarperSanFrancisco, 1990.

Foster, R. J. 1998. *Streams of Living Water: Celebrating the Great Traditions of Christian Faith*. San Francisco: HarperSanFrancisco.

Workbooks

DelBene, R. 1992. *Alone with God: A Guide for Personal Retreats*. Nashville: Upper Room

DelBene, R. 1988. *Into the Light: Ministering to the Sick and the Dying*. Nashville: Upper Room

Dunnam, M. 1998. *Workbook of Living Prayer*. Nashville: Upper Room.

Dunnam, M. 1998. *Workbook of Intercessory Prayer*. Nashville: Upper Room

Smith, J. B. 1999 (rev.). *A Spiritual Formation Workbook*. San Francisco: HarperSanFrancisco.

Spiritual Disciplines and Presence

Foster, R. J. 1998. *Celebration of Discipline*. San Francisco: HarperSanFrancisco.

Rutter, T. 1998. *Where the Heart Longs to Go*. Nashville: Upper Room

Thompson, M. 1995. *Soul Feast*. Louisville, KY: Westminster John Knox Press.

Wuellner, F. 1998. *Feed My Shepherds, Spiritual Healing and Renewal for Those in Christian Leadership*. Nashville: Upper Room.

Prayer

Dossey, L. 1997. *Healing Words: The Power of Prayer and the Practice of Medicine*. San Francisco: HarperSanFrancisco.

Keating, T. 1992. *Open Mind, Open Heart: The Contemplative Dimension of the Gospel*. New York: Continuum.

Steere, D. 1997. *Dimensions of Prayer*. Nashville: Upper Room.

Wuellner, F. 1987. *Prayer and our Bodies*. Nashville: Upper Room.

Wuellner, F. 1995. *Prayer, Stress and our Inner Wounds*. Nashville: Upper Room.

SPIRITUAL DIRECTION

Guenther, M. 1992. *Holy Listening, The Art of Spiritual Direction*. Cambridge and Boston: Cowley.

Kelsey, M. 1996. *Companions on the Inner Way*. New York: Crossroad.

May, G. 1992. *Care of Mind / Care of Spirit, Psychiatric Dimensions of Spiritual Direction*. San Francisco: HarperSanFrancisco.

Ware, C.1995. *Discover your Spiritual Type: A Guide to Individual and Congregational Growth*. Bethesda, MD: Alban Institute.

DREAMS

Hall, J. 1993. *The Unconscious Christian, Images of God in Dreams*. New York: Paulist Press.

Jung, C. G. 1968. *Man and His Symbols*. New York: Laurel Book, Dell.

Kelsey, M. 1978. *Dreams: A Way to Listen to God*. New York: Paulist Press.

Mellick, J. 1996. *The Natural Artistry of Dreams*. Berkeley, CA: Conari Press.

Taylor, J. 1983. *Dream Work: Techniques for Discovering the Creative Power in Dreams*. New York: Paulist Press.

ENERGY/BODY/MIND HEALING

Achterberg, J. 1985. *Imagery in Healing: Shamanism and Modern Medicine*. Boston & London: Shambhala.

Lawlis, G. F. 1996. *Transpersonal Medicine, A New Approach to Healing Body- Mind- Spirit*. Boston & London: Shambhala.

Myss, C. 1996. *Anatomy of the Spirit: The Seven Stages of Power and Healing*, New York: Three Rivers Press.

PSYCHOLOGICAL / SPIRITUAL THEORY OF HUMAN DEVELOPMENT AND GROWTH

Edinger, E. 1992. *Ego and Archetype, Individuation and the Religious Function of the Psyche*. Boston & London: Shambhala.

Washburn, M. 1995. *Ego and the Dynamic Ground, A Transpersonal Theory of Human Development*. Albany, NY: SUNY.